OF HUMAN HANDS

OF HUMAN HANDS

A·Reader·in·the Spirituality·of·Work

Edited by
Gregory F. Augustine Pierce

AUGSBURG
Minneapolis

ACTA
Chicago

OF HUMAN HANDS
A Reader in the Spirituality of Work

Published by Augsburg, 426 South Fifth Street, Box 1209, Minneapolis, MN 55440 and ACTA Publications, 4848 N. Clark St., Chicago, IL 60640.

Scripture quotations unless otherwise noted are from the New Revised Standard Version of the Bible, copyright © 1989, by the Division of Christian Education of the National Council of the Churches of Christ in the United States of America.

Cover art and design: Judy Swanson
Internal design: Karen Buck

Library of Congress Cataloging-in-Publication Data

Of human hands : a reader in the spirituality of work / edited by
Gregory F. Augustine Pierce.

    p.   cm.—(The Christian at work in the world)
    Includes bibliographical references.
      Augsburg ISBN 0-8066-2504-X (alk. paper)
      ACTA ISBN 0-87946-057-1
    1. Work—Religious aspects—Christianity.   2. Vocation.
  I. Pierce, Gregory F.   II. Series.
  BT738.5.O34   1991
  248.8'8—dc20   90-44647
                                            CIP

Manufactured in the U.S.A.   AF 9-2504

95   94   93   92   91   1   2   3   4   5   6   7   8   9   10

"Take these gifts we offer, the work of human hands, and make them holy."

Eucharistic Liturgy

•

"As no one is without commission and calling, so no one is without some kind of work."

Martin Luther

• CONTENTS •

FOREWORD: Confronting Dualism
William Diehl 11

PREFACE: A Spirituality That Makes Sense
Gregory F. Augustine Pierce 15

PART I
WHAT IS THE SPIRITUALITY OF WORK?

1. The Spirituality of Everyday Life
Hal Miller • Computer Systems Developer 23

2. Andy's Diner
Jeff Behrens • Priest 30

PART II
WHAT IS THE SPIRITUALITY OF MY WORK?

3. Finding the Courage to Take Risks
Frank Macchiarola • Administrator 37

4. Our Task Is to Create Worlds
Emil Antonucci • Artist 43

5. I Am a Building Tradesman
Peter Terzick • Carpenter 47

CONTENTS

6. Compassion Is the Most Vital Tool
of My Trade
Maxine F. Dennis • Cashier   49

7. From Church Job to Secular Job
Pauline Webb • Church Worker   52

8. Meeting God in Others
Kathy Petersen Cecala • Data Processor   58

9. Called to Broaden My Horizon
John Scheible • Engineer   63

10. A Monk in the Bosom of His Family
Paul Wilkes • Father   70

11. My Faith Helps with the Important Work
Mary Elizabeth Toomey Dunne • Judge   77

12. The Power and Presence of God Is
Guiding My Way
Rose Mary Hart • Letter Carrier   81

13. Finding God in Dishes and Diapers
Margaret Hebblethwaite • Mother   86

14. The Lord Catches Us in Our Craftiness
Chris Satullo • Newspaper Editor   91

15. To Walk with Each One
Cecelia Newbold • Nurse   97

16. Overbooked and Overwhelmed
Ed Wojcicki • Volunteer   102

8

17. When I Went Broke
Herman Loewen • Unemployed Worker   105

PART III
HOW CAN THE CHURCH SUPPORT THE
SPIRITUALITY OF MY WORK?

18. They Bring Their Work to Church
Davida Foy Crabtree • Pastor   113

CREDITS AND SOURCES OF ARTICLES   119

ACKNOWLEDGMENTS   123

• FOREWORD •

WILLIAM DIEHL

Confronting Dualism

A clergy friend of mine recently told the story of asking a member of his congregation who was a CEO in a major corporation to be a member of a small committee that helps the pastor each week to prepare his sermon. The committee was to meet each Wednesday evening. When he arose on the Wednesday morning before the first session, the CEO realized that he had not yet read the Bible texts for the following Sunday. So, on his way out the door, he grabbed his Bible. During a slow period in his morning office routine, the CEO opened the Bible and began reading the Sunday texts. He was interrupted by one of his vice presidents delivering a report. They exchanged brief greetings and the aide left. Later the CEO's secretary told him that when the vice president came out of the office, he had an astonished look on his face. "My God," he shouted, "What's happened to Frank? He's in there reading the Bible!"

Why is it that discussion of one's faith is taboo in the workplace? Why is it that religion is generally considered an inappropriate topic within the environment of one's occupation?

William E. Diehl is president of the Riverbend Resource Center in Allentown, Pa., and a former executive with Bethlehem Steel.

For 40 years, I have worked in the field of business. Most of that time was spent in various management levels of a major corporation. More recently, I have been doing management consulting work with small, privately owned companies. It matters not the size of the company; there are few businesses where management people feel free to talk about their deepest spiritual values.

What is true for business leaders is true for other occupational groups. My friends in law, medicine, communications, education, and other work report similarly: Matters of spiritual interest are taboo subjects in the workplace.

•

Well, so what? Isn't Sunday the time for expressing one's devotion to God? And isn't the church the place where one's spiritual life is nurtured? Why should anyone be concerned that evidence of religious commitment cannot be found in the workplace as long as people are faithful in their church attendance?

Why? Because compartmentalizing our religious life runs counter to our understanding of the Christian faith. To separate Sunday from Monday, to distinguish between the secular world and the sacred world, to divide one's life into spiritual and material compartments is to promote a dualism neither biblical nor Christian.

"The earth is the LORD's and all that is in it, the world, and those who live in it," says the psalmist (Psalm 24:1). "For God so loved the world that he gave his only Son" (John 3:16) has become a golden text of the Christian tradition. The whole world—not just parts of it—is the object of God's love and concern.

Jesus regularly worshiped and taught in the synagogue, but his ministry took place out in the world among all kinds of people: the poor and the wealthy, the powerless and the powerful, the respectable people and the social outcasts. When he spoke of the "kingdom" of God, he used such earthly examples as a lost coin, a lamp, a mustard seed, salt, leaven, wineskins, and the like. Jesus was not one person while in the synagogue on the Sabbath and another person in the world the rest of the week. He was most certainly not a dualist. Neither should the Jesus people be dualists.

So the first, and perhaps most important, reason that Christians need to connect Sunday faith and weekday life is that our biblical and theological imperatives say so. But there is another reason as well.

Christians also need to connect their Sunday faith to their weekday lives for their own wholeness and sense of well-being—for their own spirituality. Jesus warned that we cannot serve two masters. We will hate one and love the other. If we serve God only on Sundays and do not sense his presence in our weekday lives, we have set up for ourselves a destructive dualism.

In one sense, it is comfortable to be a dualist. It is not at all easy to make the faith–life connections in our places of work. It is much easier not to try. But by not trying we must inevitably trivialize our faith—for something that has no relevance to those places where we spend most of our time cannot, after all, be very important.

•

In their book, *Confident and Competent: A Challenge for the Lay Church*, William Droel and Gregory Pierce, two of the leaders of the National Center for the Laity in Chicago, point out that the models of spirituality that have been explored and celebrated by the Christian church in all of its denominations have been basically monastic. They take issue with the traditional view that one's spiritual growth can only occur when one separates oneself from the so-called "secular world."

They write: "If laypeople cannot find any spiritual meaning in their work, they are condemned to living a certain dual life—not connecting what they do on Sunday morning with what they do the rest of the week. They need to discover that the very actions of daily life are spiritual and enable laypeople to touch God *in* the world, not away from it. Such spirituality will say to the layperson worried about the lack of time for prayer: 'Your work *is* your prayer.' "

This present book, edited by Gregory Pierce, is another contribution to the development of the spirituality of work. I am pleased that Augsburg Fortress Publishers, so closely associated with my own Evangelical Lutheran Church in America, has taken the lead with ACTA Publications, based in the Catholic tradition, in beginning this new ecumenical series of books on "The Christian at Work in the World."

•

If we are to break down the barriers of dualism separating the Sunday experience from the workday experience, we need to help laypeople develop their own sense of God's call or vocation. We need to help them understand that they respond to God's call by carrying out ministries in their daily lives—in their occupations, their families, their communities, and their churches. We need to more fully develop a theology of work and focus on the spirituality of work. We need to help people develop certain skills for their ministries in the workplace. Most of these needs can be met within the structure of most congregations. Some of the specialized skills may have to be provided by other ecclesiastical structures.

But it is all "doable"!

What seems to be more difficult, however, is helping our churches to think less about institutional issues and more about affirming, equipping and supporting individuals for ministry in daily life. Perhaps the many fine articles in this book, written by men and women of faith from many denominations and occupations, will help.

Can the church be in the workplace? These reflections prove that the church already is. The Holy Spirit is at work in the awakening about the connection between faith and daily life found in virtually all Christian denominations today. Dare we hope that the religious dualism that has infected the Christian church for most of its history will someday be destroyed?

• PREFACE •

GREGORY F. AUGUSTINE PIERCE

A Spirituality That Makes Sense

"Defining spirituality is like trying to nail Jello to a tree," quipped one wag. And yet, for most people "spirituality" is what "religion" is all about. Spirituality is the search for what is eternal, meaningful, transcendent in our lives.

When I was a young man, I did not understand spirituality. I kept looking for it in the wrong places: in church, in spiritual books, in prayer, in fasting, in retreat centers, in days of recollection—in "silence, solitude and surrender."

With marriage, the births of our three children, the beginning of our own business, the maintenance and repair of an older home, and my volunteer activity in church, community, and arts organizations, however, I literally had no more time for these pious practices. It was only then that I discovered a spirituality that makes sense to me. It is the spirituality of work.

Gregory F. Augustine Pierce is past president of the National Center for the Laity and copublisher and editor of ACTA Publications in Chicago.

•

This phrase is not mine. It was actually enunciated by Pope John Paul II in his great encyclical *On Human Work*. It is a strange phrase, combining two words that I had always seen as nearly a contradiction in terms: "spirituality" and "work."

By work, the pope does not mean just paid employment. He means all of our productive daily activities—job, family and relationships, and community involvement—that help bring about the Kingdom of God. Even this concept, however, may be too religious to describe what I am talking about. To me, work is simply all human activity that sustains and improves the world. My work, then, is everything from performing my job to raising my children to tending my lawn.

Spirituality can be defined as the way we orient ourselves toward the divine. Before, spirituality for me always connoted getting away from the world. But a spirituality of work necessitates orienting myself toward the divine through my daily activity of improving and sustaining the world.

This is a radical change! No longer can I use as an excuse the fact that I am too "busy" for spiritual things. My spirituality now lies right in front of me, in the work I do most of my waking hours. As my friend and colleague Bill Droel puts it, "God lurks everywhere and everything is grace."

•

A major part of all of our lives is our work—both paid and unpaid—on our jobs, with our families, and in our communities. If work is merely a distraction from our search for the spiritual—if it is not grist for our spiritual mills—then we are correct in viewing work as a burden to be endured so that we can pursue our spirituality in our leisure time. If that's the case, those of us who spend 90-95 percent of our time "working" have a right to feel cheated, impoverished, and jealous of the monk on the mount who has unlimited time to pursue holiness. If, however, there is a "spirituality of work," then we all have an equal opportunity to pursue holiness—even sainthood—by finding the sacred in our ordinary occupations.

One word about language is important here. There are several other concepts that touch on and indeed overlap that of the spirituality of

16

work. Some people speak about the "ministry of daily life" or "marketplace ministry," others use "vocation in the world" or "worldly vocation" to describe the baptismal call of all Christians to carry their faith into their daily life. A few theologians are also beginning to develop a "theology of work." All of these phrases, while not necessarily interchangeable, seek to understand and describe the experience of the Christian attempting to connect faith with ordinary life in the world. The phrase "spirituality of work" merely emphasizes the spiritual aspect of that endeavor.

●

This is a book of reflections on the spirituality of work by people in a variety of occupations. All the articles were written in the first person and in down-to-earth, often very secular language. They show both the difficulties and the possibilities of discovering spirituality in everyday activity.

This is an eclectic collection, based primarily on my own sometimes serendipitous discovery of the material. An attempt was made to present a broad sampling of occupations, issues, and situations from a range of men and women of different denominations and faith experiences. Any imbalances that remain reflect space constraints and my own limitations.

In Part I, two articles lay the groundwork for understanding what the spirituality of work is. Hal Miller looks at the biblical basis for what he calls "The Spirituality of Everyday Life," while Jeff Behrens uses a more impressionistic and existentialist approach in "Andy's Diner."

Part II offers reflections by Christians in 15 occupations on the meaning of their work. Most of the authors are from the United States, one is Canadian and two live in England. They use a variety of writing styles: some erudite, others folksy; some using biblical or religious images and quotations, others secular; most prose, one poetry. There are, however, several themes that run through all these articles and define what I believe to be the elements of a spirituality of work.

The first common theme is the meaning of work. Is work mere toil, the "sweat of your brow" promised by Genesis? Or is work holy, a necessary part of being Christian—indeed human? People find many different meanings in their work. For some, it is "making a living"— providing the resources necessary for themselves and their dependents.

17

For others, the meaning of their work is found simply in doing a good, competent job. Others work out of a sense of obligation or duty, while some people describe their work in terms of participating in God's ongoing creation. Another experience of people is that sometimes their work is "alienating": boring, dangerous, difficult. In all these reactions to work, faith can be critical to providing a framework of understanding.

The second common element discussed by many of these writers is their relationships with others. For many, this is the central question in being a Christian at work. Workers encounter many kinds of people they must deal with every day: bosses, fellow employees, people they supervise, customers, suppliers, competitors—even fellow commuters. How a Christian deals with each of these people helps determine the spirituality he or she finds in work.

A third concern expressed in many of these reflections is balancing responsibilities between job, family, community, and church involvement. Part of a spirituality of work includes correctly integrating the various spheres of life into some "wholeness" or integrity.

Ethical considerations are also a strong component in a spirituality of work, especially in certain professions. Deciding right or wrong in specific situations, dealing with the ambiguity of the real world, deciding what good one could be doing that one is not—all these matters arise when one attempts to connect one's faith with one's daily work.

Finally, many people discover that no matter how well they do their own work, if the "system" under which they work is not functioning correctly the spirituality of their own work suffers. This leads many of these writers to reflect on the nature of the institutions of society and their responsibility to maintain those that are functioning well and help change those that are preventing them from doing their best work. The eventual result of such efforts at "institutional maintenance and change" is involvement in social justice and social action as part of living a spirituality of work.

Part III contains but one article, which addresses a specific question for the organized church. If there is a spirituality of work, and if it is critical that all Christians connect their faith with their daily work, what can the church—especially at the local parish or congregational level— do to support and promote the spirituality of work of each of its members? Davida Foy Crabtree describes the efforts of one congregation in "They Bring Their Work to Church."

•

Every attempt has been made in this book to minimize the differences and accentuate the many beliefs, practices, and insights that people of different Christian denominations share. Language was made as universal and inclusive as possible without losing the unique flavor and insights of each author.

Of Human Hands is the first in a series of books on "The Christian at Work in the World." It is offered as an introduction to the spirituality of work as well as an attempt to encourage and generate more first-person reflection by people on the connection between their religious faith and their daily work.

PART
• I •

WHAT IS
THE SPIRITUALITY
OF WORK?

· 1 ·

HAL MILLER

The Spirituality of Everyday Life

Because we lived in the country, my family did a lot of its shopping from catalogues. We had piles of them by the fireplace, and when the winter seemed to have grown too long already, we would lie on the floor and page through them. Some were large and some were small, but one sticks in my mind. It was for outdoor clothing and bore the slogan "escape from the ordinary."

I didn't like the clothes all that well, but I did like the slogan. The "ordinary" was one place I wanted out of as fast as I could go. And it even looks like that is how others feel as well. We all seem to dread the ordinary.

Our uneasiness with the ordinary shows itself in a variety of ways. Is there any city without a "Thank God It's Friday" celebration on the radio at five P.M. Friday? Why don't we thank God it's Monday? Is there a street without a car bearing the bumper-sticker "I'd rather be _____ ing?" What's the problem with doing what you usually do rather than _____ ing? Is there an adolescent anywhere who doesn't use the word "boring" as the ultimate curse on a teacher or a book?

Hal Miller is a computer systems developer and a member of the editorial core of *Voices in the Wilderness* in Salem, Mass.

We dislike the ordinary, the everyday, the routine. We thirst for the exciting, the different, the exhilarating. To put it briefly, we're "transcendence junkies." We live in the hope of some kind of excitement fix to give us meaning and vitality in a world of gray walls and Muzak. Our heroes are exciting people—athletes, actors, and adventurers—and we are so enthralled by believing they have escaped the ordinary that we never notice Andy Warhol was right: they are only famous for fifteen minutes. The last crop of Olympic champions are now working for a living just like you and me.

●

Some people try to escape the ordinary directly, through drugs. Christians are, for the most part, not quite so straightforward. We try to escape the ordinary "spiritually." We look for conferences, seminars, and revivals for moments of spiritual "high" that will allow us to move past the familiar routines of work, family, community, and church. We are after an otherworldly experience that lasts long enough to get us through the intervening days or weeks until we can shoot up the next otherworldly experience.

It is not that otherworldly experiences are wrong. It's just that we think they are the only experiences that give meaning to life. And we got that idea not from Christian faith but from the atmosphere of our culture. Modern Western cultures put an almost absolute value on the unique, the individual, the special. We celebrate the things which make us different from others and try to minimize the things which make us the same. Those of us with a lot of disposable income try to compile racks of different experiences and avoid repetition and pattern lest it become "boring."

In large part, this is a reaction—a reaction to the perceived monotony of our lives. We yearn for those special, transcendent experiences that will take us out of the tedium of sitting at a computer terminal, chasing children, washing dishes, and driving on crowded highways. We are, culturally, goal or project oriented—we value accomplishment, the feeling of being able to sit back and look at something finished. And yet most of our lives are given to tasks having no end. The furniture must be dusted only to be dusted again. The dishes must be washed so we can dirty them again. It's no wonder we are hungry for those exciting, transcendent moments.

It seems what we really want is to touch God. And we assume that touching God is exciting. But what if touching God is not always (or even usually) exciting? I wonder if Elijah was excited when he touched God in a gentle breeze rather than lightning, thunder, and tornado. I wonder if Paul was excited as he made tents in Ephesus. I wonder if Jesus was excited as he sat at dinner with people, again and again trying to explain to them that the kingdom of God belonged to the least, not the greatest. Yet these are all times when people experienced God at work in their lives—when they indeed touched God because God was touching them.

●

Maybe we're approaching this all wrong. Maybe, rather than assume that touching God is exciting, we should entertain the possibility that it is often routine, as routine as getting up in the morning and going to sleep at night.

Our Christian confession sounds very much like that. We assert that we live our lives in the presence of God, that God came to be with us in the ordinary form of a Jewish carpenter, that those who are blessed are the most common of people—the poor, the lowly, and those who mourn. Christianity offers us a spirituality of everyday life. It would be worth our while to pursue what that might mean.

Consider what everyday life looks like. One way to do this is to make a list of the activities that compose life as you know it and include the amount of time you spend at each activity. Then put the activities in order by amount of time. In my case, everyday life looks like this:

1. Working (my work—like most people's—is quite routine. As a computer systems developer, I work with words in an arcane language, words that must be written and rewritten, read and reread, dozens of times)—9 hours.
2. Sleeping—7 hours.
3. Eating (includes cooking and cleaning up)—2 hours.
4. Driving/commuting—2 hours.

5. Showering, shaving, etc.—1 hour, more or less.
6. Errands and chores—about 1 hour.

Your list will probably vary from this. In my case, the routine, everyday parts of life account for 22 hours of my average day. For almost everyone, they account for at least 20 hours. That leaves just four hours a day for everything else: chatting, bouncing crying babies, reading, television (though studies say that the average American watches TV for about seven hours), prayer, and works of service.

●

Now, think about what this means for our spiritual life. Most of the spiritualities we have received apply only to those four hours (or less) of each day of our lives *not* occupied by everyday tasks. Our Christian culture counsels us to devote time to prayer, Bible study, or ministry; we are told to attend extra meetings or do additional things. Somehow, all this is to be packed into the 17 percent of our lives not already given to the everyday. These methods of spirituality don't work that well when put to the test of work, marriage, kids, and mortgages. They do not deal with the fact that we spend most of our lives engaged in trivial, repetitive tasks of questionable "eternal" worth.

These spiritualities are backward. From a Christian point of view, spirituality should be at least as applicable to the 20 hours given to the everyday as to the four that are not. A spirituality of everyday life concerns itself with the 83 percent of our time—that vast bulk of our lives—that is ordinary, monotonous, and routine.

●

Spiritualities of everyday life have been around for centuries, but unfortunately they were often composed in keys unappealing to modern people. For 1500 years, some monks have followed the rule of St. Benedict, which required a life combining prayer and work—*ora et labora*. Both were modes of praising God, both were valuable. Other important traditions of Christian spirituality have worked toward finding the meaning of "praying without ceasing," a discipline that requires learning the integration of faith and everyday life.

Christianity, indeed, is nothing if not a spirituality of everyday life. The incarnation is the ultimate affirmation of the ordinary—God come to be with us not as a blinding light or burning bush but as a person we might walk by on the street and never notice.

If this is true, why is the spirituality of everyday life undiscovered by most of us? And why have we given ourselves to the quest for a dramatic, sensational spirituality? Some of the reasons are obvious. The everyday is, by definition, commonplace. There is little in it to get excited about. Indeed, for the most part it is invisible to us. We usually don't notice it unless it becomes a problem due to boredom. Since we only see the everyday when it is a problem, we (naturally) do not look to meet God there.

Another reason we lack a spirituality of everyday life is that our tastes in stories run to the exciting and dramatic. We like hagiography—stories of saints. And whether the saints are Christian (Mother Teresa, Johnny Cash) or secular (Lee Iacocca, Kirk Douglas), we like their stories because they are exciting. Subtly, we convince ourselves that sainthood is exhilarating, thrilling, inspiring . . . anything but everyday.

We also are bent toward the quick and easy. We want rapid conversions—not slow, painstaking transformations. We want things to be different *now*. But there is nothing quick and easy about everyday life. It goes on and on, with little closure or completeness. Everyday life is literally never done. And as a result, we look somewhere else—anywhere else—for a quick spiritual fix.

●

Yet the New Testament gives us a great wealth of resources for working out a spirituality of everyday life. Though it gives us a good share of pretty spectacular events—Annanias and Sapphira struck dead, Lazarus raised, Paul blinded and healed—its overall emphasis affirms God's work in the everyday. Jesus—God incarnate—usually went out of his way not to transcend the patterns and routines of the everyday. He made himself a friend of everyday people, including prostitutes and sinners, rather than of spiritual athletes. People called him a glutton and a drunkard (Luke 7:31-35) because he took such joy in the human

27

routines of eating and drinking. And he took his message not to the high and the mighty but to the poor (which, in that society, meant the ordinary folk).

The earliest churches were made up almost entirely of ordinary people. There were no monks, few "full-time" Christian workers (Paul even seems to have taken pride in the fact that he was usually self-supporting), and almost no one with the leisure to spend time hunting up spectacular spiritual experiences. People who thirsted for the spectacular usually ended up in the spiritually exciting "mystery cults" rather than in the boring, mundane Christian churches. The mystery cults offered exotic and secretive rituals; the churches met in the most prosaic way possible: around a simple meal.

Paul's gospel emphasized that God's work was precisely with the ordinary. "God chose what is low and despised in the world," he says, God has focused on "things that are not, to reduce to nothing things that are" (1 Cor. 1:28). This is at the root of Paul's understanding of grace: God has deliberately chosen the ordinary over the special so that no one might boast, so that we all must rest our salvation wholly in God's own hands (1 Cor. 1:29-31).

Of course those earliest Christians—like us—had a hankering for the transcendent and the spectacular. The Corinthians, for instance, had their interest in the "technicolor" gifts of the Spirit like speaking in tongues. Paul's strategy for dealing with them is instructive. He does not deny the importance of those spectacular gifts; instead he places them side-by-side with the commonplace ones (1 Cor. 12:7-11; 14:26). Sometimes, you even get the impression that the commonplace ones are more important (1 Cor. 12:22, Rom. 12:3-8).

This is but one piece of Paul's whole approach to Christian spirituality. His famous "fruit of the Spirit" (Gal. 5:22-23), the harvest of a lifetime of living in God, are the virtues of the ordinary. Paul does not expect Christian living to bring forth excellence, courage, success, and virtuosity. Instead, the Spirit brings us "love, joy, peace, patience, kindness, generosity, faithfulness, gentleness, and self-control." The spectacular never requires patience—only the routine and "boring" need this virtue. Faithfulness is out of place in transcendent experiences; only the everyday requires it. The same is true of the other virtues that are fruits of the Spirit.

●

When I am in the middle of some mundane piece of everyday life and feel the yen for escaping the ordinary, I routinely take comfort from Jesus' parable of the wise servant. The one the master finds faithful and wise enough to give responsibility in his household is the one who gives his family their food at the proper time (Matt. 24:45). Thankless, routine, repetitive, ordinary tasks such as serving a meal predictably are the ones where God finds us faithful or not. And when the master returns, the servant is blessed not because he has accomplished something special but because he is faithfully engaged in his routine (Matt. 24:46).

Faithfulness in the most ordinary tasks of life is the very thing Jesus required of his disciples. When he envisions the sheep and goats separated on judgment day, he does not think God's criteria for separating them have anything to do with the spiritually spectacular. Instead, everyday tasks—feeding someone who is hungry, visiting someone who is sick, being hospitable to a stranger—form the basis of judgment. Though the banality of this surprises both the sheep and the goats ("But Lord, when did we...?," they ask), it does not surprise Jesus. He knows full well that God's fundamental concern is with the ordinary, unimportant, and unspiritual tasks of everyday life.

Perhaps one day we will be blessed by having a fully developed spirituality of everyday life. In the meantime, we need to apply ourselves to the mundane task of working one out. I would love to see a truly intelligent, sensitive spirituality of work, or of conversation, or of meals. If we start to develop these, maybe one day we will be able to tackle the really difficult problems such as commuting . . . or sleeping.

• 2 •

JEFF BEHRENS

Andy's Diner

The name of the diner was Andy's. It was near a large industrial park, so business was always good, as was the food. The waitresses were friendly and pretty and they knew nearly everyone who came in. Andy's had an attraction for all sorts of people: rich, poor, and in between, neat and sloppy, loud and quiet, varied races, and religious persuasions.

I used to go there alone every morning and find an empty stool near the far end of the counter to better enjoy the parade of humanity.

Most did not know I was a priest. They embodied a richly textured history that unfolded bit by bit over a period of five or so years. I sensed a common something beneath all the variations, some sort of essential goodness that drew people there and seemed waiting to be told.

•

Andy has since died and the diner is now boarded up. I was honored to offer his funeral Mass. Perhaps his passing and the closing of the diner has prompted me to write of the goodness of Andy and his diner, for they offered more than mere food.

I asked Andy's wife if I could have a small, glass ashtray with the name and address of the diner. It is more valuable to me than all the

---

The Rev. Jeff Behrens is on the staff of Our Lady of Mount Carmel Parish in Montclair, N.J., and teaches at Caldwell College.

Waterford in the world. I felt liked there, and in turn I truly liked the people who filled the place each morning. They seemed unaware of the wealth of raw and unadorned beauty that their lives and words were.

The place so fascinated me that I went through a period when I would be the first one there, as early as five in the morning. Jack, the short-order cook, went through a meticulous routine of arranging his food and wares for the coming day. He was a friendly man, slender, fast at whatever he had to do. He could handle five or six breakfast orders at once, never losing track of their sequence. I hope he is well these days. His health had started to fail toward the end of my stay. He was missing from Andy's funeral several years ago.

•

I was pursuing graduate studies and would stop for lunch on the way to class. There was a waitress who worked the lunch-hour shift, young and attractive. One day she told me she noticed my books and school papers. She said she, too, was going to school, trying to get her college degree by going part-time. Waitressing helped her pay tuition and care for her baby. She was divorced and had a difficult time making ends meet. I asked her what she hoped to do after receiving her degree. She said she loved writing and hoped to become a published author.

The next day, she brought in one of her essays, a piece about her former husband who was wounded in Vietnam and had suffered flash-backs after returning home. I found her writing so moving, but she never spoke as openly as did her writing.

If I could track her down, I would ask her to write about those years. The most fertile soil is our memories and our loves. Only they can make us grateful. Only they are capable of causing us to feel joy and sorrow. We suffer only from what we have known, from what has deeply touched our being, as those in the diner have touched mine.

•

There was a professional photographer there every morning, in his late thirties, generally healthy looking. He was chatty with Jack and Andy, talking about his family and business. One Monday morning, he was missing from his usual seat. Jack kept the seat empty, not wanting to disappoint him should he arrive.

31

By Thursday, there was still no sign of him and by then his seat was almost always taken by a newcomer. The next week, the photographer's body was found in his car several miles from the diner. The police judged his death a suicide; he had blown his brains out with a shotgun. He had left the house that morning, the last morning of his life, saying he was going to stop at the diner.

•

Chelsey used to operate a garage across the street from the diner. He was usually the first to arrive after Jack opened for business, shortly after five. He was bald, short, fat, grimy, and smelled like the garage. He was divorced many years ago. It was not hard to tell that he might be a difficult man to get along with.

Chelsey had a repertoire of the funniest but raunchiest jokes I have ever heard. At first, he did not know I was a priest. Someone must have told him, though, because one morning he acted very sheepish when he came in. He proceeded to tell Jack about the poor condition of the buses.

I felt bad about his change of demeanor, but gradually the conversation between him and Jack became so boring that he again came around to his old and perhaps better self. He died not too long ago. There were no services—he was estranged from his family, and most of his friends had died off. He died alone in his small living quarters attached to the garage.

•

Andy was a good man. Many poor people traveled by bus from Newark to the many factories in the area. It was not unusual for some of them to stop into the diner and ask Andy for food or money.

He was softhearted. After a lecture on the meager state of his own resources, Andy would ask Jack to prepare a take-out breakfast and would place a five-dollar bill on the little tray before Jack wrapped it up. Those people were often forlorn, forgotten, lonely. They needed someplace where their lives could be given value simply because their stories and troubles were listened to.

Andy also had an agreement with the warden of a nearby jail. Upon the release of an inmate, Andy told the warden, he would be willing to offer a job in the kitchen until the released person could find a better means of income.

•

I truly loved the people in that diner, and a generosity of spirit that was so much a part of it. Christmas had such a beautiful meaning there. Andy would decorate the diner with strings of lights and artificial snow from an aerosol can. The diner took on a magical glow and there was a heightened sense of the incarnation.

It was a place in which God himself would have felt at home. Those who frequented Andy's impressed me deeply with their earthiness and their gutsy coping with the harsh realities of life.

I believe God had a special affection for that place. God would have enjoyed every tale of woe and promise and found something of himself in each person there. Their lives were such a potpourri of goodness and wisdom, tempered by the brute numbness of factory labor and the unfairness of the way things are when the lack of power and money afflict human life.

There was something sacramental to it all. Those people gave me something that made me think about and long for the truth and experience of God. I cannot describe the feeling of profound peace I knew on those mornings when I would arrive before dawn, sit at the end of the counter and meditate. Seeing the milkman come in, then Chelsey, then the local police officer, reminded me how we are all drawn to some essential goodness in life, and that place somehow had it.

•

Can organized religions learn something from that little diner? Religiosity certainly was not explicitly there in terms of language and ritual, but it was there. What used to get my wheels going was the perception of institutionalized holiness that those people carried with them as a part of the "worldview." Whenever a topic came up that involved the bantering about of God or church, I could pick up feelings of indifference, disappointment, or anger. Institutionalized faith did not mean much to them and had somehow alienated them.

In my heart, I know their feelings were nearly accurate. A significant dimension of the church had removed itself from their experience. They looked at and resented—indeed felt betrayed by—pious attitudes, abstract or removed concerns, clericalism, and at a root a resistance to living in the real world, their world.

They were and are the world of labor, of nonrecognition, of commuters, diners, bus stops: the world that the institutionalized religious concern attempts to convert by exhorting and sermonizing, and yet a world that provides the fresh and raw life from which religious meaning must draw its sustenance for reflection. It is the world from which we all "emerge" and a world religious specialists would do well to remember.

•

If the church does go bankrupt in terms of personnel and cash, I would suggest that it collapse into diners all over the country. Bishops, remaining priests, gurus, ministers, rabbis, and swamis could find spots at counters across the country and just listen, feel welcome and be friendly.

There would be no dead rectories or manses to return to, nor would there be the need to return for ceremonies because there would be no congregation. They could go to work, to offices and factories, to schools and garages, to banks and computer terminals and discover one another in diners.

And please, do not seek to impose sacred words or sacred rituals in such places. They are already there. No need to "point out" the religious significance of diners. That seems to function best when left unaddressed.

PART
• II •

WHAT IS
THE SPIRITUALITY
OF MY WORK?

• 3 •

FRANK MACCHIAROLA

Finding the Courage to Take Risks

All too often, our lives are caught up in so much doing—and so little thinking about what it is that we do—that when we do reflect, it's usually because some outside force in our life brings us to a moment of truth. Modern life sweeps us along, and often our family and colleagues as well. Before long we are acting out of instinct. Our relationships become almost automatic. We take others for granted and ourselves too seriously.

I believe that the modern world encourages and supports the development of lives without reflection. People suffer a great deal because of their failure to reflect upon what has the most meaning in their lives. Having despaired of the ability to discover truth because we cannot be scientifically certain of things, we all too often abandon the search. We have, in short, missed out on much of the practical beauty of faith.

This phenomenon—of a life caught up in a rapid swirl, and the failure to search for deeper meanings of right and wrong—poses the greatest difficulty for public figures in America today. In public life we become consumed by ourselves and by the significant power that comes

Frank Macchiarola is president of the Academy of Political Science, a professor of business at Columbia University, former chancellor of the New York City school system, and president of New York City Partnership.

with an office of public trust and responsibility. We become accustomed to seeing matters of "right and wrong" and "good or evil" in personal terms. "Right" means those who agree with us, "good" is what we support. Our enemies become the "evildoers."

The most difficult thing I have had to do as a public official in pursuit of the "public virtue," justice, has been to remind myself that enemies can be right and that their point of view might even be better than my own.

For example, on several occasions when I served as chancellor of the New York City Public School System I was forced to rethink positions I had taken—on issues such as confidentiality of student records, high school admissions policy, and testing—when student advocates took exception to the bureaucracy's policies and practices. I found myself having to fight the tendency to refuse to listen because I took exception to the speaker, or to the way in which the case was being pressed.

The tendency to blend the "good" with my own position and the "right" with my own beliefs and values has been a problem I have sought to overcome. And nothing has been more antithetical to the position that I believe is correct than this political axiom—an axiom that has become a standard of political action and reflects the arrogance of power: "Don't get angry, get even."

•

I have come to understand better the meaning of political arrogance and the real limits of political power when I have taken time away from the pace of business to think, to reflect, and to pray. Prayer has been a part of my adult life, and it has often led to a change of mind and a different course of action. For me, prayer with others has been most meaningful as part of a dialogue in which the search for a sense of right doing has been a central part of the endeavor, where the search for an answer has shaped the effort to do the very best we could. Very often, those who have prayed with me have not even realized that I considered what we were doing to be prayer.

Frequently, as schools chancellor, I called upon my staff to discuss what we should do on matters affecting our youngsters. Should we implement a promotional program that might hold back tens of thousands of pupils? Should we accede to a court order involving the evaluation and placement of youngsters with handicapping conditions? I needed the answers of my staff to such basic questions, and I needed those answers to be based on honest judgments about what the staff thought was right and wrong. I relied on my key staff to speak not on the basis of the bureaus they administered; I needed them to affirm their belief in youngsters. These meetings I considered prayer. And I treated the honesty of my staff with great respect. I believe my administration of the schools had its credibility because these persons had provided it through their own integrity.

Prayer has occurred oftentimes because I needed to make many tough decisions: choosing among candidates for appointment, determining priorities of the organization, deciding what the possibilities could be, whether the setting has been reflective enough, and whether the discourse has been focused on right doing. The influence of prayer has been clear to me, and the participation of others in that search for wisdom has been partially responsible for its effectiveness.

•

The influence of prayer into what I do is basically the same for me as both a public figure and private citizen. I decided many years ago—when I became an adult—that public and private life were one, and that virtues I sought to practice would be the same for me whether I was alone, with my family, or with the larger community. I decided as well that my faith in God had to be lived in every experience and in every way possible, and that distinctions between public and private standards were wrong for me. I can't really explain why I made these decisions or what the process was that led to them. But I have spent a great deal of my life trying to figure out what is the right thing to do, and I guess it seemed easier and certainly better to have one set of guiding principles that I could apply in all situations. That underlying principle is that you treat people—all people—with dignity and respect.

I have learned that spirituality knows no denominational boundaries and that the common experience shared by many of us in America today involves a faith sharing that makes the meaning of a religious community and a church far more inclusive than rules of the organization would suggest. Indeed, anyone in public life who searches for kindred spirits limited to one religious denomination is defeating his or her own purpose. I have been disappointed too often by those who define the church in terms of whom they can exclude. I have been encouraged by those who, if they cannot share the faith, share its possibilities and its potential. I believe that by fashioning an inclusive church we will evangelize in the most fitting way for 20th-century America.

●

Another of my basic assumptions has been that most people are unaware of how wonderful they are or can be. The idea that people can do a great deal more than they are doing, that they can be saintly, is something that is strange to far too many people. And I believe that the failure to understand our capacity to be good is at the core of our failure to perform as successfully as we might. It is this faith in humankind that, I believe, represents my own personal contribution to others when I am operating most effectively in Christian witness. For example, this belief in perfectibility has led me to encourage individuals—students as well as my own children—to believe in themselves and in their capacity to know and to do. Often it is the only way I get them to broaden their own horizons or to accomplish what they consider the unattainable.

When I was chancellor of schools, I established a practice of taking two students with me whenever I went on speaking engagements or meetings out of the city. This gave me the opportunity to talk to the students, and invariably to challenge them to do more with their lives. I challenged one girl, who ranked third in her high school class, to choose a college that would stretch her intellectually and not to settle on her initial choice. Five years later, as a Wharton School graduate, she attended a speech I gave to a group of accountants in New York City and reminded me of a trip she and another student had taken with me to Washington, D.C. Another youngster whom I met by chance in Manhattan, told me that the trip he accompanied me on—just a breakfast meeting at Gracie mansion (residence of New York's mayor)—gave him a greater sense of himself. He had seen that he had a place at the table with the city's "big shots." The best phone calls I have ever gotten have been on Father's Day from youngsters who thought it was appropriate to call.

Many teachers' success with children stems from a belief in the youngsters' dignity, in their God-like qualities, and in their understanding that God expects saintly things to come from them. It is this belief in children, when acted upon in the classroom, that reflects the tangible evidence of a faith at work. Too often we are afraid to draw on this relationship and to acknowledge that our work with students is not only a job, but serious and fundamental work that is related to our own basic responsibilities as Christians.

●

Another assumption that I have come to operate on is that most people (and society itself) do not understand the difference between things trivial and things consequential. Our society regards dealings with others as trivial affairs. In highly structured corporate or political cultures it seems virtually impossible to give as much respect to the receptionist and clerk as to the vice president, chief executive officer, or chairman. And yet, I believe that such equality of respect is a necessary part of what we should be about in the process of living a good life. I believe that in many ways our social interactions should give evidence of our belief that we are one community and that God has a very real and immediate closeness to every one of us. This lesson applies strongly as well at home for family. I learned at St. Francis College, from a sociology professor who later became a good friend, of how the concept of true community goes far beyond what we see around us in the various social organizations we loosely term "community." The requirement of community-building—in family life, in social life, and in our civic life— requires an infusion of personal commitment that combines a strong sense of self-worth with a strong sense of how the larger community must operate in basic harmony.

At certain times I have felt quite lonely pursuing what I thought was a basic part of the community's value system, only to find out that many people were unaware of what I was talking about or what I actually meant. I tried to start a junior ROTC program in high school because I thought students should have that option. Every staff person at the meeting opposed it. They thought the military should not have a presence in school. I used them to be my conscience. I felt often that the education community largely refused to understand the basic entitle-ments of children. Caught up in the politics of the possible, the pro-fessionals of public education seemed too willing to defend the fact that the school setting frequently denied students some of their basic rights as individuals. (I brought a lawsuit against the board of examiners—I was on the board—and won the point that found discriminatory the test for supervisors in the public schools. Few women or minorities had ever been chosen.) Poor teaching, poor use of instructional time, low expectations, inadequate curricula, and an uncaring atmosphere were all too often defended on the basis of the needs of the system. Instead of protecting children, conventional wisdom often would have us believe that adults must be protected from children.

At the same time that we trivialize the important, we make im-portant the trivial. In these situations we confuse the importance of a job with the importance of work. We think that leadership is only a function of those endowed with leadership roles in complex organiza-tions. Such a respect for power is, I believe, misplaced. It promotes ambition and measures success in terms of potential rather than ac-complishment. In public life we define a life of success in terms of higher office. Why not regard real success in terms of the broader view of work, and appreciate and honor those who do well all manner of work?

•

It is the power of prayer, as well, that affords us courage to do things that are filled with risks. And here is where I have come to value my faith more fully. The ability to do things that I believe in—to push for a program, to advocate an unpopular cause (like integration in a world that rewards elites)—has required the insight and strength that prayer affords. I believe that my faith in God has mattered a great deal in the quality of the work I do.

•4•

EMIL ANTONUCCI

Our Task Is to Create Worlds

The most intense perception of my childhood, undiminished after 50 years, was that everything of consequence in life is hidden: God, the sources of art, the workings of our bodies and minds, the forces of nature, the heart of another human being. One had, somehow, to live with these mysteries. Even the simplest and humblest of things partook of mystery. God was there, hidden in the world of appearances, but somehow not separate from them.

So, I became—as all artists must—obsessed with appearances, with the very "thingness" of the world, with looking constantly and carefully at the world, certain that if I made the right visual connections in the constantly shifting patterns of both the world and my own mind, I would see. See what? The being of things, I suppose. But I have never been satisfied with the notion of art as a revelation of meaning or as the communication of meaning. I see art as the creation of structures, the creation of worlds that meaning may inhabit, but not define. That's why great works of art last. Whatever the original intentions and meanings invested in them by their creators, they continue to provide structures that can be inhabited by successive generations.

Emil Antonucci is an artist and instructor at Parsons School of Design in New York City.

•

I see the way art works as an analogy for God's presence in the world. People create structures in the mind, in society, that God can inhabit. It is a task that—like the artist's—depends not on theories and explanations, but on the skill with which they are fashioned: life as skill; art as skill; the experience of God as skill. All require unremitting awareness—a kind of constant scanning—just below the level of consciousness, the ordering of myriad small currents of the mind. Without this skill, some inevitable law of spiritual gravity drags us down and away from the reality of God's presence and reduces us to rote definitions of God that have no life.

Our task, as believers, is to create structures of ourselves skillfully enough that they can be inhabitable by God—in the way that art and music can invest a cultivated sensibility. I see prayer as this skill. Prayer is less petition or communication than this daily structuring of our minds to permit God's entrance. I see spirituality not as some force lurking behind appearances, but as the perception and even creation of a pattern in appearance—the figure in the carpet, always present, but unseen until we order our vision.

In a word, I don't think skill is the prerogative only of the artist. As film director Jean Renoir once said: "Art is not a calling, but the way in which one exercises a calling, and also the way in which one performs any human activity. Art is making." All human beings possess high orders of skill, progressively diminished in industrial societies. The individual experience of making something, whether a shoe or a painting, from start to finish, must somehow be regained in a society where most of us are the passive users of the skills of a few others.

•

Anyone who makes things in the sense I speak of knows that something works through them, waxing and waning without their control, that only a kind of faith and constancy of belief will get them through. This experience of making something forms the "grammar" of religious experience. Without it, I believe, our notions of God become too mental—not actual enough to inform our daily lives, and too "personal" to enable us to share the experience of God with others.

Whatever God is, God is a totality, a wholeness that connects the world and ourselves, the past with the present and the future, the living and the dead. The great appeal of the visual arts for me is that approximation of the experience of totality, of everything happening everywhere at once. Literature and music must take place in time, but a painting gives you a whole world in the instant you see it. At best art is only an analogy for this sense of God's totality, but it does exercise all the right mental and spiritual muscles. The notion that artists are "divinely" inspired is presumptuous and sentimental. All human beings participate in the continuing creation of the world. The artist's skill is simply the paradigm of the process. This process is a constant one of reconciling the random events of daily life with the spiritual values we maintain, of integrating the contradictions inherent in everyday life. Artistically, it is safe in our time to deal in fragmentation and disassociation. What is difficult and full of risk is to create images and structures of wholeness, integration, and harmony. I don't think we understand enough about the era we live in to make convincing images of wholeness. Our era is like the cinematic effect of the "dissolve," that is, two scenes—one fading away, one coming into being—caught at that instant when both images are of equal strength. We who come to consciousness at that instant cannot say which elements of this composite image will fade, which will endure. This ambiguity runs through all our lives. It is the prime characteristic of our art and our religious lives.

•

It is this fragmentation and ambiguity that make the creation of "religious" art so difficult. People with the same religious beliefs may still have very different sources for their images and symbols of the world, since these images are largely formed by the dominant culture, which is clearly not religiously motivated. The working artist who is trying to shape his or her work in the artistic values of the time may face impossible contradictions between high art and popular art, modernity and tradition, the private symbol and the public one. Such contradictions account for the prevalence of religious art that is either "popularly" sentimental or vaguely nostalgic for the art of some "religious" era.

45

We need to recreate the very definition of religious art. My own sense is that the best we can expect from believing artists is the patience to wait, to pursue their goals of wholeness in their work in solitude until we, as a society, can find our way to some degree of integration and harmony. I suspect that in some complex and confused way we may even be moving away from the notion of the artist as an exclusive occupation, to a wider participation in the making of the symbolic structures we inhabit. The pressures from all the forgotten ones of the earth, from the cultures excluded from the dominant white Western culture, are not inexorable. The development of the interactive computer video, capable of drawing on a data base of all art of the past and mingling these images, opens incredible possibilities of wider participation in the making of art. And as crude as these developments may appear to be at the moment, they offer the hope of escaping the "commodification" of art and healing the split between high art and mass society.

•

I feel no conflict between artistic solitude and my concern for society. I feel sure that all the hidden forces of the world interconnect as much as the overt ones do, that our task is to create worlds that sustain the mystery of God's presence, not resolve it. Our task is to hone the skills that enable us to live in a world that will always be full of contradiction.

In my early teens, crossing the bridge from Brooklyn to Manhattan over a dark, dank East River one wintry morning, I watched a patch of reflecting, golden light move across the water beneath me. It suddenly struck me that the entire river surface was at once both dark *and* radiant—depending on one's angle of vision—but clearly both. I still don't know the "meaning" of that image, but I have never lost the feeling of its power: the reconciliation of contradiction, the embodiment of both appearance and inner reality . . . God around us, within us—impenetrable darkness/radiant light.

·5·

PETER TERZICK

I Am a Building Tradesman

I am a building tradesman.

My hands are custodians of skills a thousand generations old, held in trust for a thousand generations.

My predecessors created the Hanging Gardens of Nebuchadnezzar and patiently put together the Parthenon.

My successors will construct platforms in space and way stations on the stars.

I harness the rivers, bridge the inlets, disembowel the mountains, and level the valleys to make the nation strong in war and prosperous in peace.

The mightiest skyscraper begins with a stake I drive in the ground and ends with the turn of the owner's key in a lock I install.

Between the stake and lock I fight searing summer heat and bitter winter cold.

Danger is my constant companion and instant death lurks around every corner.

Peter Terzick was the retired general treasurer of the United Brotherhood of Carpenters and Joiners of America in Washington, D.C., and the former editor of the *Union Register* and the *Carpenter.* He died on July 1, 1990.

The astronaut begins his probe of the heavens from a launching pad
I build.

The mightiest surgeon performs his miracles in an amphitheater I
erect and provide with heat, light, water, and technical
equipment.

Even at the birth of the atomic age one of my brothers* was there.
And when the first test proved successful, Enrico Fermi, the
master scientist, placed his arm around the shoulders of this
brother and said: "Gus, with all our education, what could we
have done without your experience?"

I stand straight and walk proud, because I know my contribution to
society is based on skill, not bluff; on sweat, not sweet-talk; on
production, not press-agentry.

I am a building tradesman, belonging to a building trades union.

Because I am, I need truckle neither to king nor tycoon.

---

*The first atomic reactor was built at the University of Chicago. The atomic pile was
actually put together by Gus Kauth, a member of Carpenters Local No. 1922.

· 6 ·

MAXINE F. DENNIS

Compassion Is the Most Vital Tool of My Trade

Cashiering in a supermarket may not seem like a very rewarding position to most. But to me it is.

You see, I feel that my job consists of a lot more than ringing up orders, taking people's money, and bagging their groceries. The most important part of my job is not the obvious. Rather it's the manner in which I present myself to others that will determine whether my customers will leave the store feeling better or worse because of their brief encounter with me. For by doing my job well I know I have a chance to do God's work too.

Because of this, I try to make each of my customers feel special. While I'm serving them, they become the most important people in my life.

•

Sometimes a sincere smile helps me to achieve this goal. More often than not, however, it takes more effort on my part.

Maxine F. Dennis is a cashier at a supermarket in Coventry, R.I.

Recently, an elderly man came to my register. I sensed immediately, by the expression on his face, that he was lonely. I wanted to brighten his day. But how? I wondered. He had failed to respond to my smile, nor had he replied to my genuine greeting of "How are you today?"

As I began to ring his order, I spotted a box of birdseed. It was then that I knew I had found my opportunity.

"Oh, I see you have a pet bird too. Aren't they fun?" I asked.

Suddenly a warm smile appeared on his face. Then he began telling me all about his parakeet.

"You know, that little fellow is real company to me since my wife, Mary, passed away six months ago."

"It must be difficult to cope with the loss of a loved one," I commented thoughtfully as I placed his bundles into his shopping cart.

"It certainly is," he sighed heavily. "We were married for 50 years, my Mary and me," he added, his eyes twinkling brightly from her memory.

"How wonderful. Please come back and visit with me soon. I really enjoyed talking with you today," I told him as he started to leave.

"You bet," he answered. I noticed that although the loneliness on his face was still there, it had diminished somewhat.

My heart felt light because I realized that I had done something worthwhile that day. I had taken a few minutes to care and listen to a fellow human being, succeeding in making at least a tiny difference in this one, precious life.

●

Sometimes I find that simple acts like the way I bag the groceries—or place them in the shopper's arms or shopping cart instead of sliding them to the edge of the counter for him or her to pick up—tells that customer that I care and respect each person as an individual.

●

Observation and perception are the two tools I use most often to do God's work while doing mine.

When I detect by the hassled expression on a customer's face that her day has been less than great or realize that she must be in a hurry by the way she keeps glancing at her watch, I try to help her by working as fast and efficiently as I can. Because I sense she's tired, I'm careful to bag her groceries lightly, keeping related items together so it'll be easier for her to put her things away later.

Compassion, however, is the most vital tool of my trade. There are many sad stories to be heard while ringing up grocery orders. Many times I find I'm called upon to help nurture the emotional state of shoppers—just as the food they're buying will provide nourishment to their bodies. Hearing of death, terminal illness, fatal accidents, and broken homes is all part of my job. During such times I try my utmost to listen with my heart, not just my ears. Often a single word of understanding or a mere look of genuine concern is just the right dose of medicine to help heal a bruised heart. When I succeed in easing some of the pain of another human being, it is then that I realize just how important my job as a simple cashier is.

•

The rewards I reap from my job far exceed that of my weekly paycheck. The real rewards are invisible and intangible. They are the warm feelings that penetrate my soul and the personal satisfaction at the end of my working day. It's these that assure me that I have done God's work and have done it well!

· 7 ·

PAULINE WEBB

From Church Job to Secular Job

For the largest part of my working life, I was an employee of the Church in Britain. I always regarded myself as singularly fortunate in having a variety of fulfilling jobs and in working in what I thought must be a unique atmosphere. My colleagues created a community of committed and concerned people whose dedication to their job made up for quite a number of disadvantages in the actual conditions of their employment. Moreover, through a whole committee structure of consultation, I came into contact with people from many different walks of life, who nevertheless were actively interested in the projects I was engaged with and whose advice was always actively sought and seriously considered.

The fact that my professional life spread into others' leisure time seemed an inevitable part of being engaged in what the rest of the world regarded as a "vocation" rather than a "job." This seemed to mean that we worked without any sense of such mundane limits as set hours, agreed salaries or clearly defined areas of responsibility.

I confess, however, that from time to time I felt a certain embarrassment about it all. For one thing, I found that "professional Christians," if I may describe me and my like thus, at times reacted strongly

---

Pauline Webb is a former officer of the Methodist Church–Great Britain and is head of religious broadcasting in the World Service of the British Broadcasting Corporation.

---

against the idea of applying professional criteria to our work. Because we were working in a field that relied so heavily on voluntary and lay assistance, we seemed to think it inappropriate for us to lay claim to any special skills ourselves. We felt obliged to delegate responsibility for decision making to others. This meant we had to attend countless committee meetings that moved in concentric circles of representation, so that we kept meeting the same people discussing the same issues at different levels of decision making.

In addition, there was a complex network of interrelated, inter-church, interfaith, international meetings—all engaged in the task of coordination and cooperation, and concerning which one felt a great burden of responsibility for reporting back to one's base. Here, ironically, the fact that I was in church employment and therefore technically available at a time when other lay people would normally be working meant that I became involved in more and more church committees. The majority of these seem—somewhat incestuously—to depend upon "professional" lay people's time to make up the laity component in meetings geared toward suiting clerical working schedules.

•

Another cause of embarrassment was related to our actual working hours. We seemed to develop an enormous guilt complex about having any time off to pursue our own amateur interests. I remember once meeting a colleague out on a Saturday excursion with his family. When I congratulated him on choosing such an excellent way of spending his free time, he immediately leapt into a defensive explanation that this was his first free Saturday in six months, that usually all his weekends were spent "on the job," and that even now it was an unexpected cancellation that had made the outing possible. My own schedule similarly fettered me to engagements two or even three years ahead of time. Only by the subterfuge of planning for what I wrote in my appointment book as "home missions" could I keep any dates clear for myself and my private life.

The most embarrassing area of all is related to money. Each time I took up a new appointment in the church, I found it difficult to discover exactly what I was going to be paid. Not that I was excessively concerned about that; I knew I would be treated fairly. But it was just that it seemed to be one of those difficult subjects people preferred not to discuss, as though there were something disreputable about even raising the question. And even when the basic rate had been made clear to me, I still found that when it came to matters like extra expenses encountered on the job, there was a certain diffidence about mentioning the matter.

I still cherish an early memory (the currency indicates how early) of a journey I made on church business to what seemed then a long way away. "How much do we owe you for your fare?" asked the treasurer. "One pound, three and fourpence," I replied. "Well," he commented, "we're not worried about the odd pence, are we?" and generously handed me exactly one pound.

•

Such was the unpredictable, friendly but somewhat precarious atmosphere in which I spent the larger part of my working life. So, when at the age of 50 I announced that I was considering applying for a job in the so-called "secular world" I was warned by many friends that I would miss the warm womb of Mother Church and find myself in a world of hard competition, keen negotiation, and clearly defined chains of command. I confess that I did feel nervous about joining the staff of a huge institution, where I was immediately given a staff number, a contract, and a book of rules. Moreover, I was encouraged to join a union—a new work experience for me. It seemed that I had now come into a realm where law, rather than grace, abounded.

I was soon to discover, however, that the regulations were designed to build into the structure of my job those aspects of colleagueship that I had always valued most. But this was all within clearly defined limits, which in an unexpected way proved to be most liberating in their effect.

For example, in my church job I heard a lot said about "pastoral care," but never did I find this kind of care built into the actual provision made for those who were in full-time professional employment in the church. I suppose it was expected that church workers would receive support from our own local clergy—even though the very nature of our job made it difficult for us to be closely associated with a local congregation . . . and for those ordained ministers fully to appreciate the particular dilemmas of our daily work. Consequently, there rarely seemed to be anyone with whom we personally discussed our own immediate responsibility or who helped us make an assessment of what we were achieving professionally and to evaluate our own strengths and weaknesses.

When I first learned that in my new job such an evaluation process went on regularly—with regular reports being written and then discussed with one's superior officer—I became quite alarmed about it. But I discovered that this was to be a most helpful, objective, analytical exercise that I had never been part of before. In addition, I was to find that all matters relating to my personal affairs were the concern of a special department whose advice I could call upon with no sense that I was imposing on someone else's time or goodwill.

Instead of all these people keeping an eye on me, as it were, I soon discovered the enormous amount of delegated responsibility I was expected to carry in a clearly defined job. Although there is a clear chain of command in my secular job—and everyone knows where the buck stops—very little buck-passing actually goes on because each person is expected to shoulder the proper burden of his or her own responsibility and to "refer up" only those matters on which there is genuine doubt or difficulty. Similarly, although provision is made for such consultation processes as ensuring the sharing of specialist knowledge, the clear demarcation of who decides what and when makes unnecessary that whole mesh of coordinating, cross-representing committee work that once took up two or three days of every working week.

When it comes to the mundane matters like money, expense accounts, time off or overtime, all embarrassment has gone. Everything is set out clearly by agreement or negotiation in an open and objective way that seems to me more humane than the overzealous sense of commitment that drove some of my former colleagues to the point of breakdown. In secular employment, one is protected not only by concern for one's own interests but by what seems a healthy concern for the whole body of the institution—which is prevented from making impossible demands upon any of its members lest it incur the wrath of corporate strength.

Probably the difference I noted most of all between secular and church employment was that in the former I have found much greater emphasis on and therefore priority given to the immediate end product of the job. I suppose one could say that this, too, is a matter of definition. A secular institution employs people for quite specific purposes, usually spelled out in a clear job description and measured in terms of actual productivity. In church circles it is much more difficult to say what the end product is.

One of the temptations of working based primarily on our religious commitment is that we are tempted to take such a long view of things that we sometimes miss seeing clearly the immediate task. There were some church jobs I held—such as that of an editor—where deadlines were clear and work reached regularly a point of completion. In some of my later responsibilities such as "lay training," however, we seemed to spend an inordinate amount of time discussing our long-term objectives—leaving us too little concentration on producing short-term results. (That may have been my own fault as well as that of my committee!)

Yet this does not mean that I now miss entirely the longer view of things. One of the warnings people gave me when I left church employment was that I would miss the stimulus of discussion with kindred spirits who shared my faith and my outlook on life. One of the surprising things I've found in a much more mixed working environment is that I get involved in far more theological discussion than I ever did before . . . and the stimulus of having one's basic Christian assumption challenged is quite exhilarating.

•

Inevitably, therefore, all this new experience has led me to review what we mean when we talk about "lay training." I remember many years ago being puzzled by a lay person who said at a training conference, "When I hear people saying how much they look forward to Sunday, when they can come to church to get away from the tough demands of the outside world, I want to reply that I look forward to Monday, when I can go to work and get away from the tough demands of the church."

I think I have glimpsed now a little of what that man meant. Secular institutions have a lot to teach the church about how to legislate for liberation. By that I mean how to ensure that people are not overburdened or guilt-ridden and asked to carry more than their proper

load of responsibility, about how to recognize the diversity of special-
izations and gifts that people have, and about how to delegate appropriate authority.

If I now had some responsibility for lay training, I would approach
it not from the point of view that the church has everything to offer
lay people in helping them relate their religious faith to their daily jobs
but rather that there is also a secular wisdom learned in daily work
which people might be encouraged to relate more fully to their life in
the organized church.

· 8 ·

KATHY PETERSEN CECALA

Meeting God in Others

At those times when I think of the laity, I don't always think of myself as being a part of that huge and diverse group. I think of teachers, doctors, nurses, social workers—people whose workaday lives involve some "worthy" human contact. There is some potential in those occupations, I think, for affecting the lives of others in a positive way—winning grace through the practical application of the commandment of love.

But behind my computer, as an indexer for the nation's foremost business newspaper, there seems little opportunity for my faith to play any sort of role in my work, which deals primarily with the world of money: the intricacies of corporate finance and international exchange rates. I plod through industrial-production statistics and over-the-counter listings and other dense data; and only through the occasional insider-trading scandal, or when some hapless arbitrageur goes berserk, does that dark "real" world of unpredictable human beings reach my computer screen. Even then, they are disposed of swiftly, converted into bytes and characters that glow briefly in amber, before I dispatch them—with the flick of a button—into the system's memory: an odd nether region I imagine as a sort of "computer purgatory," where all those

---

Kathy Petersen Cecala is an indexer for the *Wall Street Journal* in New York City.

nuggets of information, names and numbers lie suspended in darkness, waiting to be brought back to life on someone else's screen.

When I enter my office building each morning, part of the huge World Financial Center complex in New York City, I feel that I'm stepping into a secular cathedral; the cold marble floors, lofty windows, and hushed atmosphere evoke an unmistakable church-like feeling. The elevators, with their dark paneling, seem like confessionals, and I often have the uneasy feeling that I've exchanged one religion for another.

And I am, to be truthful, attracted by it all. It's very fashionable, trendy—still—to be involved in big business, and there's something seductive, compelling about the great game of Wall Street, megamergers and hostile takeovers, as well as the staggering, unreal amounts of money it all involves . . . and what that money can buy.

And yet, probably because of my strict Catholic upbringing, it's a fascination I feel guilty about—like a sexual perversion of some sort, something forbidden and ultimately wrong. I worry that my growing fascination with money and business—and accompanying sense of materialism—is impeding my spiritual growth, setting up roadblocks in a path already filled with enough dips, twists, and turns to last a lifetime.

•

Actually, there is little chance that I will be sucked into this world of greed, power and desire. The work I do is not that exciting. While it concerns money, I have no contact with any, other than my weekly paycheck. Rather, I deal in information storage and retrieval, and so I find myself in the cold, inhuman world of statistics and dates. At times the job is challenging and fascinating, but it leaves me somewhat isolated from the world of people.

And I find that people are essential to my spiritual growth. That is where I find God—not in my computer screen (despite what some popular novels might have me believe), although the sheer complexity of the world I record dutifully each day suggests to me the workings of a much higher being. I often mourn the fact that my work does not bring me into closer contact with fellow humans, but it does, at least, propel me outward when work is over. My husband—who works as a graphics artist, alone at his drafting table without much human contact as well—and I are active in our community and civic groups; we have strong ties to both our families and make an effort to strengthen friend-ships, some of which date back to childhood. But I find myself con-tinually looking, seeking out more opportunity for connecting and shar-ing.

•

Seeing the corporate world on the scope that I see it in my everyday work—broken down into many, many tiny fragments and facts and intricate detail—gives me an interesting perspective on life. Just as I sort through vast amounts of data, trying to pinpoint what is essential, what is valuable, so too does my life—as a busy commuter, as a wife, as a Christian—present myriad moments and experiences that must be sorted through to determine what is meaningful, what is important. And sometimes there are incredible moments when I can actually feel God's presence, moments of light interspersed among the gray and everyday. These I consider tiny miracles—"miracles" in the most basic sense, from the Greek root, *mira*, to wonder. Moments to wonder.

An example, and this is an obvious, easy one: Sometimes I go to Mass on my lunch hour—if for no other reason than to get out of the office, to get away from the relentless glare of my computer screen, particularly if my workload for the day is heavy and dull. I don't always go to the same church, and there is something profoundly moving about hearing my voice blend in with those of strangers around me, in response and in song. There is the exchange of the sign of peace, turning to take the hand of the person beside me, or in back—perhaps another office worker, a Manhattan laborer. A stranger, and yet for a fleeting moment, the briefest second, our eyes meet and something passes between us, evident only in a faint smile of recognition, a slight bit more pressure in the handshake. We are special, you and I; we share something in-credible.

•

Of course, churches are great settings for little miracles. What's harder— a much bigger challenge—is meeting God outside church walls. It's very difficult, for example, to feel much love for humanity when I'm crammed into a rush-hour train. My fellow Jersey commuters as a whole are an affluent but obnoxious lot, and there I am, jammed into a corner with someone's Rolex stuck in my face, another's Louis Vuitton tote stuck in my ribs, while the fellow next to me moans to his companion about taxes on his $300,000 summer home, or the unavailability of parts for his antique auto. But small miracles occur, even here.

One especially hectic Friday evening, midway under the Hudson between Manhattan and Jersey City, I sensed a weight pushing against my shoulder. Suddenly, the handsome, pinstripe-suited, and very, very pale young man next to me sank to the floor of the train. After a brief second of shock, dread, or fear, everyone in the crowded car took action, as if we'd been organized beforehand. At once, everyone moved back, and several people stepped forward to loosen the man's tie and gently stretch him out; someone else pulled the emergency cord and others went searching for a conductor or doctor. I remember a palpable sense of hope as everyone waited, silently, for the man to be revived. There were no jeers, no remarks of anger or disgust—only quiet concern, hope. Everyone seemed to be holding his or her breath, waiting for an eyelid to flutter, some sign of life. When the young man finally did manage to rouse himself and sit up wobbly, there was a collective gasp, some applause, and chuckles of relief.

This incident, when I think of it, still astounds me. When the train pulled into Hoboken, everyone dispersed, disappearing into the crowds, united only for a few minutes by a simple human drama.

•

The streets of the city offer many such moments when another person enters our lives—however briefly—and changes it, sometimes subtly, almost imperceptibly, other times in more dramatic and permanent ways. I cannot forget the one winter evening, several years ago, when I darted out across Broadway on a green light and the heel of my shoe abruptly snapped, sending me sprawling into the path of oncoming traffic. Before I could even react or gasp, a man whose face I never saw scooped me up and swept me over to the other side. He hurried away, a tall hunched figure, before I could even thank him for possibly saving my life; indeed, for risking his own.

Sometimes we get to play the savior, too. Once I was approached by a somewhat shabby, elderly woman who greeted me with a hug and a strange greeting: "Lydia, how nice to see you again!" I was about to shake her off, thinking her senile, when I noticed lurking behind her several unsavory looking characters. I quickly escorted her into a store, where she told me the men had been following her for several blocks, taunting her. When the coast was clear, I walked her to her destination, and I still remember her tearful gratitude.

These are special moments. They involve making a quick decision, a choice that reaffirms our faith. But even less dramatic moments are special, too—some so quick, so fleeting, you could miss them if you blink or look away. Anytime I connect with someone else in a positive way, I feel good. For example, teaching a coworker some complicated task on the computer: I show her and show her and show her, but she doesn't get it, can't get it. Then suddenly, "Yes!" Or I see someone I had met at a seminar seven or eight months ago, and she greets me warmly, with recognition, even remembering the story I had told her about my mother-in-law.

•

Simply put, I find I meet God in others—in their love and concern and attention. And though my particular job at this time involves little contact with others, it does send me outward to seek out this essential contact. There are enough of these moments to convince me that God's love is present always in our lives. Like Anne Frank, I believe that people are basically good at heart, and I believe it even though I have always worked in New York City and lived in the crowded, busy, industrial Northeast. I believe this even though I read continually of evil and corruption and injustice, even within the few city blocks in which I work. I believe, because there is always one small moment, some small miracle that occurs, to give me reason to hope.

•9•

JOHN SCHEIBLE

Called to Broaden My Horizon

Perhaps the greatest constant in the midst of so much change in my life is the beneficent presence of others. I'm a self-motivated, independent person. But without relationship, the fallacy of independence is painfully clear. My view of God is influenced by this realization. My strengths, hopes, and accomplishments stand on the one hand; my needs and blessings received appear on the other.

Certain images, adjectives, and roles have formed my self-image at different points. This self-image defines how I see the others in my life. That these images change with time seems obvious, but still it is something I'm struggling with. These images are extremely powerful ways the Lord touches me at given times. When they change, they indicate I am moving on to new horizons.

•

In high school, my predominant self-image was "athlete." People looked to me as a talented player and leader. I had always done well at my studies, but the image of student or scholar didn't motivate me yet. Playing ball was the real thing.

John Scheible of Rochester, N.Y., is a practicing engineer in a large chemical company.

About that same time I began to have questions about my faith. What's in this for me? What religious images mean something to me here and now? Because of the example of my family and friends, I had a definite sense that the answers to those questions would be important for me.

Perhaps the best illustration of my questioning was my reaction to the Nicene Creed. This creed was very troublesome. I stopped repeating it blindly, with no clue as to what it really meant. Yes, there were folks who said: "It means what it says. It's that simple." Yet it didn't seem so to me.

●

Shortly thereafter, I attended a university and found the image of student and scholar becoming more and more meaningful. Learning actually became fun.

My freshman year I stumbled into a great course in theology. The first book we read was *Church Dogmatics in Outline* by Karl Barth. It's a fascinating view of the Apostles' Creed, one that stirred me to re-examine and develop my own view. The entire experience—the book, the students (and new friends), the professor and teaching assistant— was an unexpected delight.

As an engineering major at a large university known for its liberal arts heritage, I loved to surprise people with my strong interests in music, art, history, and theology. Engineering faculty were puzzled when I took more courses than recommended, especially when many of them were in liberal arts studies.

Eleven years later I find many more images that motivate and to some extent describe me: engineer, pilot, pianist, tennis player, boy-friend, and believer.

●

Today I work at a multinational chemical company as a chemical engineer. My specific job carries the title "project engineer"; I am the team leader of a group of technicians and engineers. We work on specific installations of capital (equipment and machinery). The goal is to provide a manufacturing unit capable of producing certain chemical products safely and efficiently within a fixed budget and time frame.

The project engineer is the one team member who has responsibilities beyond his or her technical area. We communicate the technical scope and cost to management for approval, organize the team and focus it on the mission ahead, write status reports at various critical times, define and maintain interrelationships between the people in different disciplines, and define tests that ensure the facility has met the objectives and all legal requirements. Sound boring? It very rarely is. It's the responsibility inherent in the job that causes the greatest satisfaction and excitement, but also occasional nagging pains in your gut and some sleepless nights.

The dangers of explosions, fires, and lethal gas leaks are familiar to all practicing chemical engineers. It is our job to analyze the risks in a certain design and to reduce them to an "acceptable" level. How low is low? We often have to figure that one out for ourselves. Then we have to argue for that analysis and solution. We make it our own and commit to it.

It takes time, money, expertise, and commitment to reduce risk successfully. The project engineer, as the spokesman and center of the team, is challenged at every stage of the project life. If you are successful, you are assigned larger and more complex jobs. If you're not, you go looking elsewhere for employment, at the very least.

•

How does the theme of the presence of the Lord through others appear in my work? What self-images or roles am I being influenced by today? I had a mentor when I first arrived. He was the guy everyone loved being around—full of good humor, interested in you right here and now, eager to teach and to learn. He had a twinkle in his eye that showed his zest for life. People saw it and were drawn to him.

He never told me what to do on my projects. When I thought I had a solution, he pointed out that it had limits and conditions. There were more solutions, some even better than mine. He taught the importance of teamwork, of gaining the respect of others, and of "bridging the gap" between the engineers in different disciplines. When I would share my frustrations over the shortcomings of others, he would smile and say, "Unless you've walked a mile in my moccasins, don't get on my back!" He was a wise man.

He had just experienced a divorce. The experience affected him—the cigarette smoking, the beer gut, the disaster area of a desk. Yet he never dwelled on his problems. He had a very positive outlook on life.

One time, I ran into trouble on a project. There was a "rush" job that had to be installed "now." (Beware of the rush job!) I was told by my boss at the time: "No need to ask questions, son, just install it, dammit." The technical details of this project involved containing pressures of over 4000 psi. The operation was inherently dangerous. My analysis showed the potential of developing much higher pressures in a big hurry.

Looking back on the experience, my foes—most of whom were older and very suspicious of new technology and engineers—take on a warm, humorous look. I remember the famous cartoon character, Foghorn Leghorn, walking up to the little rooster (me in this case) who was reading a book on how to design a new and better trap for a "chicken hawk." Foghorn's response showed his proud contempt of a new concept and young roosters: "Boy, I say, boy, I say whatcha got your nose in that book there for, son?" But this experience was no cartoon. The boos were very real, and my boss (alas!) was leading the chorus.

My mentor saw the problem, but could offer no technical solution. The resolution was my job. But he did help enormously by encouraging me to search for data to support my hypothesis, for others with experiences with similar systems, and for technical journal articles. With some effort, I came up with a credible alternate solution to the design question.

The short-term consequences of my persistence were not pleasant. I had gone from budding young "star" to "bum" almost overnight. I took a beating at the "polls"—the next performance review. But I did learn to (1) analyze and communicate clearly the risks associated with a given design; (2) obtain supporting data; (3) seek out help from others; (4) propose a design up to my standards; and (5) stand by that view. Better to take the heat now than to install a machine that doesn't work or—worse yet—hurts someone.

The personal element is often overlooked in engineering. The presence of real commitment, positive encouragement of fellow workers (and especially from those with seniority), often creates the atmosphere necessary for positive results. The ability to buck the flow, when supported with adequate data and theory and alternatives, is critical. Yet technical complexity across disciplines, potentially dangerous processes and equipment, and business pressures often create a very different climate. The inquiry in the Challenger shuttle disaster posed just such an atmosphere: senior people putting on the "business hat" (also referred to as a "frontal lobotomy") becomes an excuse for neglecting expert opinion and data. The presence of others in positive ways can't be overstressed.

•

Not long after our collaboration on the rush job, I learned from my mentor that he had just been diagnosed with a brain tumor. The next few months were nightmarish for him and his family. I remember seeing him in the hospital a short time later and being shocked by the sight.

He came into the office during a brief remission to say hello. Actually, he was saying good-bye. At one point he broke down and cried. What a shock to the everyday mood of the office. I shudder as I remember the moment—the sense of unease at how little I could comfort him and how utterly useless my offer of prayer seemed. It felt so empty. I never saw him again.

The funeral was surprising. They read his poetry. Poetry? It was a poem of a hunter and a deer, of nature and beauty and life. What a transforming experience. I forgot my loss as I wondered at how much more he was than what I knew. Even in death he (He?) was teaching me that my views and thoughts and feelings are often so very narrow. I miss him now and remember him in the words of the psalmist: "As for mortals, their days are like grass; they flourish like a flower of the field; for the wind passes over it, and it is gone" (Psalm 103:15-16). That passage hits me a little too close for comfort.

The psalms tend to describe feelings, moods, and situations with which I can identify. There's a sense that this material is unfiltered by kindly bureaucrats wishing to save me from difficult theological concepts. The psalms individually and collectively move me more powerfully than any other book.

The psalms speak to me, also, in my piloting experiences. How I love flying. I feel like a kid does when he knows he's having too much fun. Each flight brings new challenges and beauties. The scenery and perspective dazzle and enchant. Changing weather fascinates, surprises, and sometimes terrifies me.

Early in my student pilot days, I took a flight with an experienced pilot and friend. We had been flying for about an hour or so when the visibility and ceiling began to diminish slowly. We radioed the flight service station for the latest local weather and radar report. "All clear" was the answer. So we pressed on, reassured and confident. A lightning bolt at 12 o'clock changed all that. The pilot let out a howl that seemed to be heard for miles. I was too shocked to make a noise.

We found out later that we had tangled with a severe thunderstorm, with cloud tops over 45,000 feet high. I found my friend's reaction rather humorous. The guy with the "right stuff" suddenly was on the verge of tears! He sure didn't look or sound like Chuck Yeager (then again, neither did I).

Life often seems to treat us like that. There's always something there to surprise you, to jolt you out of your complacency, to show that your hopes and dreams and your very life itself depend on so much more than one can imagine. "All your waves and your billows have gone over me. . . . My help and my God" (Psalm 42:7, 11).

•

Which brings me to the church. Actually, I have been describing what I think of as church. It is people in their everyday lives: basketball players, students, professors, engineers, pilots. And yet it's so much more than I can see just now. My horizon goes on just so far.

I am fortunate to attend a church where this presence of people in all their wondrous display of talent, joy, anger, and peace is accepted. It seems to me an acceptance that reflects the attitude that we all need each other and have something to learn from and to give to others. It's an acceptance of personal limitation, but also a powerful image of a church that cannot be described totally or even most appropriately by words, pronouncements, and orders. The people do it so much more elegantly by their lives. Theologian Bernard Lonergan wrote, "Religion in an age of crises has to think less of issuing commands and decrees and more of fostering the self-sacrificing love." I think the people who are the church already recognize this.

Such a lack of clear distinction between what might be called the sacred and the profane may seem puzzling and in need of clarification. Am I disdainful of laws, decrees, and authority? Do I not believe all the commandments and strictures in the Scriptures, pronounced more or less accurately by the "official" church? Is there no difference between the church and our secular lives?

My experience as an engineer and a pilot is telling on my answer. My career and life depend on my respect for and knowledge of law. To flaunt laws carelessly is to court disaster. But I also know that laws need to be applied to the here and now, not by an Einstein or a Thomas Aquinas, but by me.

In fact, my life cannot be fully explained by laws and decrees. There are too many variables, interactions, and surprises. My horizon includes the standard "church" elements, but that is a subset of a greater arena where the Lord meets me. Images of what I might be, people with their love for me, and the Lord call me to broaden my view and horizon. I hope I'll be up to the challenges.

· 10 ·

PAUL WILKES

A Monk in the Bosom of His Family

Not that long ago, I spent a year as a hermit, one with a special intention and a goal. My life at the time, although outwardly successful and certainly free, was hollow.

I wanted something more, something to give myself to beyond whatever article, book or film I was working on at the time, beyond whatever worldly pleasure I had a hankering for at the moment.

I had long been attracted to the Trappists and had spent many a week and weekend at St. Joseph's Abbey, outside Spencer, Massachusetts. If any part of my life at the time made real sense, it was my time at Spencer.

●

So I abruptly told the woman I was dating (and constantly breaking up with as I knew that a simple marriage would never satisfy my deepest yearnings for a true life's vocation) that she should consider me permanently out of her life. I cut my moorings, rented my New York City apartment and found a tiny house not far from the monastery's back gate.

Paul Wilkes is an author and film maker in Gilbertsville, Mass.

My objective was simple: I would live as much of the monastic day as possible at St. Joseph's and otherwise perform my *ora et labora* (prayer and work) in the solitude of my hermitage, set on a poetically isolated and wind-swept hillside.

I tried very hard to become a Trappist during that year. I wanted to hear a call more than I can remember wanting anything in my life. I was sure my life then would not only have meaning, but would also make enormous sense and, certainly, be most worthwhile.

But, at year's end—after so many hours of prayer and meditation, hundreds of masses in the great abbey church, fasting and selected mortifications—it didn't happen. I loved the life of a "pilot fish monk" I was living. So much about the monastic life was absolutely right for my temperament and needs. I wanted the Trappist life full time, for the rest of my life, but somehow it didn't want me.

Not that I was rejected, for I never formally applied. It would have been foolish. That important connection was never made. The falling in love or hearing a call or whatever form in which a vocation is manifested never occurred.

I left the hermitage, slowly regained my secular bearings and, to the shock of the woman I'd been dating, proposed. She, in turn, shocked me by saying yes. Like most mortal men, I married. Like most husbands and wives, we had children. And now, looking back to the religious life I so badly wanted, I smile. Little did I know God would answer my prayers in due season and in a divinely selected venue. Little did I know that the monastic life was only a wedding ring away and that the insights into monastic life I'd had in the year at Spencer would be refocused (and only slightly refracted) in married life.

•

I offer some notes from my diary that year in the hermitage—and some recent revelations.

> The monastic day is ideal; nothing goes on for too long, neither prayer, work, nor worship. My life has been too open-ended; I had time for everything and for nothing, really. I need this kind of discipline; I wasted so much time, got so little done before, and I was so flabby about such simple things. Yes, monasticism has the answer for me! (February)

I thought I knew discipline at Spencer when I methodically allotted time to prayer, reading, physical work, and my own writing. I discovered true discipline when I had not the mandates of Holy Benedict ruling my life, however, but those of Holy Noah and Holy Daniel, now nearing ages four and two.

Nap time, meal time, the thickness and absorbency of a diaper—Benedict should have only known such parameters. Now I must carve time for spiritual reading and other mystical pursuits out of those hours before HN and HD rise or after they go to bed. Now, my writing is done in intense blocks of time, morning and afternoon when the house is somewhat quiet or when an emergency run to the pediatrician or pharmacy isn't required.

Even my outdoor work is ruled by things such as Noah's naps (no chainsaw or tractor noise allowed—he'd want to get outside immediately; Daniel would sleep through an earthquake) and the boys' attention span in picking beans, shoveling snow, sweeping the barn. My work hours are never open-ended. I have built-in governance.

Yet, as I found in my hermit days, slicing the day into digestible portions brings a freshness to each part. More can be accomplished in eight one-hour segments than in one eight-hour marathon. (Painting is the exception to this rule. We have many shabby rooms awaiting such marathons or the sale of the movie rights to my two unpublished novels.)

•

Giving up my will is absolutely essential. I was much too willful before, steered by the rudder of my own foolish, immediate, seemingly important needs. Now I rise at an hour my body says is impossible, sit in meditation for periods I could never have endured before. I look for opportunities to have my will broken and for my spiritual director to tell me to forget this, not to pursue that. (April)

Basically, as a married man with children, I have no needs. My will is a soft, sweet memory placed in the album of my mind on the afternoon my wife and I drove up in front of our house and reached into the back seat to bring out seven pounds of baby and the seventeen pounds of blankets in which he was swaddled.

Now I not only rise at odd hours, but rise continually, hourly. Fever and assorted viruses, teeth coming in, coughs and misplaced blankets—

all conspire to break up a night's rest. Where, in my days of monastic aspiration, I could rise at three A.M., build a fire and doze–meditate on my Zen kneeling bench, my thoughts on Aelred of Rievaulx, John of the Cross and Teresa of Avila, I now must be, at any hour, of steady hand and sound mind, if not body, as I plunge a thermometer between tiny, hot thighs, measure the Tylenol to exactly the 0.8 cc level, change a diaper using pins that, in the faint nightlight (to put on the lamp would mean even less sleep) could inflict not only pain, but resentment—and therefore more sleep lost.

After supper, I've found, is a particularly purifying time. Even as an ersatz monk, I relaxed with the newspaper (and so do many of the Trappists, by the way). But no more. Not mine, but thy will be done, Holy Noah and Holy Daniel. You are unwinding from the day; you want to climb on me, dump out all the toys you own; you want a book read, a hug administered, the connections behind our frost-free refrigerator explained. You want to take your shoes off, you *must* put them on immediately as if the battered green rug in the playroom had sprouted slivers of glass.

And then, finally, there is that delicious moment when baths are over, toys put away, supper dishes washed, floor hosed down and the last drink of water requested and supplied. Daddy (a.k.a. Almost Monk) slips into bed with magazines with strangely yellow corners and distant dates, that book by a dear friend who keeps asking my opinion, and assorted fliers on such diverse subjects as—my range was always awesome—new Rototillers with power takeoffs and Individual Retirement Accounts (not only do I have no needs, I discover after seeing my accountant each year I have no future). I fluff up the pillows behind me and snuggle down beneath the comforter.

I awake with a start some hours or minutes later—dictated, of course, by the need of others—buried in paper as those poor chaps in the O. Henry story. Onto the floor goes the night's reading to be reheated on the morrow.

●

The closeness of the monastic life is absolutely right for me, not at all claustrophobic. Learning to get along with certain monks, whether

I like them or not, is a blessing. These are not like the disposable friends I had; I can't trade them in for a new set. (June)

The monastery, although it seems to be a study in closeness and community (oppressively so to some who have actually been taken away in straitjackets), is but a tea dance, with oft-changing partners. There, next to you in choir, is Brother A; for your morning's work in the Holy Rood Guild, Father B; for lunch, taken in blessed silence (of this I cannot write in my current life, lest I cry), Brother C. Study in scriptorium, work in the kitchen, a chapter meeting: D, E and F.

Now I have the same faces all day, every day, faces dirty and smiling, defiant and pliant, demanding and acceding. And I must love them in all their mutations. Not *like* them, be mindful, you can *like* a dog or even a fellow monk, but you must continually *love* your children. Remember: gifts from God, divine mysteries, fruit of your loins and so on. And besides, without parents such as we having our way with one another, they wouldn't be here in the first place. Our product. This one you can't pass off.

While I am mentioning something of my wife (whose cause for canonization will be forwarded to Rome soon), I must add that she, too, is present to me all day, every day. This is the free-lance writer's life. Only when I am wrestling with my IBM PC am I unfaithful. Every meal, every morning, every cleanup. Nose to nose separating Legos from puzzle pieces, wooden blocks from plastic, at the clothesline, in the supermarket. I'd wanted the Old Monasticism and gotten the New Marriage.

And then there is bed. Of course, more togetherness. Those poor monks, forced to close out the world and lie in their quiet rooms, blissfully alone, to feel no kick when a murmur issues from down the hall, not be catapulted out at a shriek in the night. Who would wish for such deliciously lonely nights as the monks must endure?

●

There is no escaping from yourself in the monastic life. As Abbot Thomas Keating says, "Ours is a vertical, not a horizontal life." Just what I need. I was always moving on when a situation got stale or predictable or no longer gave me the payout I wanted from it. I've lived too long on the surface of life; now I'm going deeper. (August)

"I can not go on!"

I have wailed, muttered, sobbed, and raged this line. No one listens to my anguished plea. I used to feel like a rolling stone; now I am so vertical I feel like I will reach my molten core at any hour. I am tested daily, extruded and pounded, overextended and overwhelmed.

I have patience Job would covet. My voice at the spilling of the third glass of extremely sticky orange juice is that of Mr. Rogers. My calmness at the tangle of tape hanging from the cassette is that of a medieval mystic gazing at a sunset. My fist softens and I administer a pat on the head for the help my son has given me in turning an afternoon's writing into the hopeless garble on my computer screen.

And there is no chance of escape.

I have children who cry if they are not fed and who will want to wear clothes of continually larger sizes for most of the next two decades. They will want me to read books to them and tie shoes for not a few years. They will not be satisfied with 12 years of education, and then I will really be purified.

I have taken a solemn vow before God to live until death with one woman. I told her father the same thing. He is a very good lawyer who wasn't sure about me in the first place. I would not want to talk with him in court.

•

I have companions along the way now, people who are after an ideal that is so worth striving for. I stand alone before God, I know that, but I no longer feel alone. All I need do is look down the line of faces in the choir stalls or beside me in the woods as we chain saw and split, in the scriptorium as I do some research among the monks who are quietly reading. I can be part of 1300 years of tradition. I can take to a path many have walked before and many will follow after. (October)

At St. Joseph's, those companions might grab your elbow as you stumbled along the path to holiness, but would they kiss your head after you bumped it for the third time on that sagging beam in the shed? Would one of them take note, as you came out of the bathroom, and say in the same tone as you have said it and yet not be mocking: "I'm so proud of you for going potty." Or would a fellow monk volunteer

"I sorry" for so simple an infraction as dropping a half-gallon of 1987—a bad year, and therefore expensive—maple syrup onto the wide-plank flooring, with its ready, capacious spaces yawning between the planks?

Would any of them be so poetic and sure in their faith as to begin, in your presence, their night prayers with "Dear God, I know you love me so much."

Thirteen hundred years! A grain of sand in the great hourglass of time. With marriage and children, we're talking Adam and Eve.

Who can ever feel alone in the Grand Pursuit again? We are after the same ideals: the opening refrain of the Sesame Street theme song, a good peanut-butter sandwich, a car ride for an ice cream cone, a walk through the biggest puddle.

●

As much as I want to be called to this life, I'm not. But if this isn't for me, what is? What will become of me: will I just go on searching and never finding? When will I know when I've found my "true" calling? (December)

With the marriage vows, I took my simple profession—with the birth of the first child, my solemn. This is a lifelong commitment. For certain, there is no need to worry, at least for the next 20-odd years (and I hear they don't even leave you then). By then, I'll be close to 70. I wonder if our Social Security checks will be bargaining chips if I ever try to persuade St. Joseph's—and my wife were to convince the Trappestines at Wrentham—of our delayed vocations.

I'd best be careful, though, if I had any distant dreams about retiring to the monastery and serenely living out my last years. The extraordinariness of my spiritual growth as a married man would surely prompt them to want me to immediately serve as abbot.

· 11 ·

MARY ELIZABETH TOOMEY DUNNE

My Faith Helps with the Important Work

My job as an administrative law judge is to determine whether people who have claimed an injury at work have been treated fairly under the law, and—if not—to provide an opportunity to remedy the situation. As an administrative agency, my "court" is part of the bureaucracy of state government. I have to balance the judicial need of the people whose cases I hear with the statistical and other bureaucratic needs of the state. I am assigned an average of 69 cases a day, which means that I have five minutes for each person to come before me and receive the justice that the system provides.

•

I decided in the fourth grade to follow my father's footsteps into a law career. I saw that the work he did had value and meaning—not only in his life but also in the life of our family. My mother was a homemaker who often relied on Mary Reed Newland's book, *The Year and Our Children*, in setting a religious tone in our upbringing.

Mary Elizabeth Toomey Dunne is an administrative law judge for the New York State Workers' Compensation Board in Albany, N.Y.

The vocations of my parents set the example for me that spirituality and faith are integral parts of the decision not just to have a career but to follow a vocation. The living example of their religion and work had a profound effect on me in choosing my profession.

●

My first case as an attorney made clear to me that the law is not just a profession of forms but of substance. As the newest associate in the firm, I handled the initial interview of a woman seeking a divorce. As we progressed through the divorce process, we sought temporary alimony for her from her husband. I wrote to the attorney for the husband with a simple message: Pay soon or we'll see you in court.

My letter was mailed on Monday. By Thursday, the attorney had received the letter and met with his client to discuss payment. On Friday night, I was advised that our client's husband had committed suicide.

It took me a long time to get over the feeling that I may have played a role in that man's death by sending what I thought was just a form letter.

Our firm handled the estate. I had to minister to my client, a woman who not only blamed herself but was accused by her in-laws of causing the suicide of her husband. Law school taught me how to handle the necessary paperwork, but it was my faith that helped me do the important work.

●

I remained in general and workers' compensation practice until the opportunity arose to become an administrative law judge. I applied for the position as the natural progression of my career. I'm happy I did, but the fact that I consider my work a calling has not lessened the difficulty of balancing my Christianity with what often appears to be the impersonal bureaucracy necessary to maintain a state agency.

My daily focus is what my friend and colleague Charles DiSalvo calls the first step in being a Christian lawyer: courtesy and competence. I expect this not only from those who appear before me, but from myself as well.

•

I've had some good experiences. One woman was very upset. She lived in an area where there are few lawyers and even fewer who regularly practice in the workers' compensation field. She had a tough case. At her hearing I was not at a bench but at the same table with her. She started to cry. I reached out and took her hand. She calmed down, and I went on to the other 68 cases I had that day.

I later learned from one of our social workers that my hearing was the turning point in that woman's case. She told the social worker that if the judge could take the time to hold her hand, then there must be something good about the system despite all of her frustration. She finally went out and found an attorney willing to learn enough about workers' compensation so that her case was resolved in her favor.

•

There are so many people coming through my courtroom that it is easy to simply label them as a number on the calendar. Rather than allowing this to happen, I try to write down birthdays, anniversaries, or other information that can personalize the hearing.

On the back of my nameplate on my desk is taped the prayer of St. Teresa of Avila:

> Let nothing bother you
> Let nothing dismay you
> Everything passes
> Patience gains all
> God alone is enough

This prayer reminds me throughout the day that it is only with God's support that I can fulfill my call to be Christ-like in all that I do.

•

In an effort to reach and maintain high professional standards in my court, I often point out errors in the files assigned to me. One of my colleagues who is responsible for the people who prepare my files reminded me that her staff handles more than 30,000 files a year. If only 1 percent have errors, she pointed out, it will still be a large number just due to the volume of cases. Yet maybe, she said, we need to recognize that 99 percent of the work was correct.

I realized that she was right. In our effort to improve performance, much emphasis had been placed on the negative—the failures, the errors, the imperfect. There seemed to be few pats on the back or acknowledgements of the jobs well done.

As a result, I began a "Pollyanna Diary." Just as Pollyanna forced the minister to locate all the joyful passages in the Bible rather than dwelling on the fire and brimstone ones, so too have I accepted the challenge to accentuate the positive.

At the end of each day, I now write down what was done right—saying hello to someone in a special way, deciding not to berate someone for a mistake, or personalizing a case. Two colleagues and I now meet regularly to support one another as we try to infuse this positive philosophy into the work we do within our agency.

•

I'd like to say that when people walk into my courtroom they can immediately identify me as a Christian jurist by my actions. I do not, however, always deserve such recognition. I feel my shortcomings as a jurist very deeply because they represent my inability in a given situation to respond as Christ would.

When we accept the challenge to integrate our faith with our work lives, however, we must also be prepared to deal with failure as a Christian as well as failure as a worker.

Sometimes, however, the rewards for making the effort can be sweet. In attempting to personalize the case of a candy salesman not long ago, I mentioned to him that I had been to the candy factory of his company. I complimented him on remaining slim in the face of all the temptation his work provided. My hearing attendant had also helped the man locate a tie tack he had lost during his medical examination. The gentleman thanked us and left.

An hour later, a case of candy was delivered to the hearing room for all of us to share while we waited for the end of a long day of hearings. Jesus would have liked that.

· 12 ·

ROSE MARY HART

The Power and Presence of God Is Guiding My Way

It was a day of great joy when the Postal Service called me for a job interview just two months after I completed high school. At the time, my main reason for wanting to work for the Postal Service was that it was outdoor work and a job through which I could meet a lot of people. Little did I realize how God was preparing me for a lifetime of special service in and through the people and events that constitute a career as a letter carrier.

From the very beginning, I worked hard on punctuality and efficiency. These are sources of pride for letter carriers. I also quickly realized how dependent people are on such service—especially the elderly and the shut-ins. I would acknowledge the greetings of those I passed on the street, but very rarely would I say anything else. Being a rather shy and quiet 18-year-old trying to learn how to handle the adult world of everyday work was difficult enough.

This style of work lasted for the first seven years of my career. Through all of it, God was laying the groundwork for my future ministry

---

Rose Mary Hart is a letter carrier for the U.S. Postal Service in Wheeling, W.V.

---

by establishing a relationship of trust and dependency among the people I served as well as the crew I worked with. This trust was the key that opened the way for my later involvement in what is now my local church. Because people knew me from work and trusted me, they began to accept me in areas of church ministry that had previously been closed to women—especially women under 25.

•

One event set the stage for me to connect faith and work in a vital way. I had started praying with a charismatic prayer group, and as my search for purpose and meaning in life continued I began to look for other ways to grow in my relationship with Jesus. I was invited to make a "Cursillo," a weekend retreat that focuses on living one's faith in one's daily life, and it was a profound experience that totally convinced me that there was a new way to live and relate to all I did. I still remember very clearly how I stood up at the closing Mass of the Cursillo and said, "There are two ways to carry mail: You can carry it. Or, you can *carry it!*" From that day on, life for me as a letter carrier has been changed.

I now see my overall supervisor as the Lord Jesus. He is present and active through the regular supervisors and postmasters. I feel an accountability to the Lord for how I do my job each day: Have I done my best for all concerned: bosses, people served, myself?

•

I believe that Jesus has given me a mission to proclaim him to all in faith, hope, and love. No longer do I wait for others to greet me on the route. I try to greet them as soon as I see them, and keep abreast of their personal situations such as illness, a death in the family, or some special honor.

I find a special joy in the grade-school children who walk a block or so with me on their way home from school. They share their joys and sorrows of the day and also take a special interest in what I'm doing. In essence, these children are my adopted ones, since I have none of my own.

I have been a regular on my particular route for eight years now. This has led to much deeper relationships with the people I serve. They remind me so very often of God's love. One hot August day a few years ago, I saw a car stop in the middle of the street. I thought maybe the driver had car trouble. No, it was someone on my route. She was traveling home from the grocery store and just stopped in the middle of the street to give me a Popsicle.

Another hot day, I was working the block around the town swimming pool. I heard someone calling me. When I turned around I saw a friend's 2-year-old trying to pass me a half-melted ice cream bar and a glass of pop through the fence. This act of kindness became a weekly treat for both of us.

Even on the coldest days God has manifested his love for me through a note in a mail box here or there asking me to ring the door bell. My first thought is that someone has a question about mailing a letter. But often I find someone taking a hot chocolate or tea from the microwave, just for me.

•

The Lord also provides many opportunities for evangelization. Many of my patrons live alone. Most of these are elderly. As a letter carrier, I may be the only person someone will see on a daily basis. This is where punctuality is so crucial. So, too, is the greeting I have for these people. In just the few short seconds that I have with someone, I need to try to hear what they are saying and respond in love and faith. At times my best and only response may be to offer to pray for them. Sometimes I can hear the family chaos through the closed doors of a house. Then, too, a prayer is needed on the spot.

Prayer can't stop there though. Prayer is necessary at the beginning of the day to put things in the proper perspective. It is a total surrender to God's will for me. It is necessary throughout the day as well, in asking for help in dealing with situations or people, in praise of creation, and in thanksgiving for opportunities to share Jesus' message by being who I am, and where I am. Prayer must continue at home after work also. It is there the Holy Spirit may direct me to further action on behalf of someone I met during the day.

As my life with the Lord deepened, I often wondered if I could somehow manage to receive Jesus daily in the Eucharist. I used to feel disappointed that there was no church locally that offered Mass at a time that didn't conflict with my work schedule—except during Lent.

Now I realize that I do receive Jesus daily through each day's people and events. In this way, I share a communion with my brothers and sisters. This is a strong source of hope and strength. Even though life can seem lonely at times, especially when I am faced with taking a moral stand, I know that Jesus is with me and present in the others I deal with.

This helps me to look beyond the people I may disagree with when decisions are made that affect my job as a letter carrier. My faith helps me in dealing with issues such as productivity, employee working conditions, and customer service.

•

The more I reflect on the gospel and current church documents—such as the U.S. Catholic bishops' pastoral letter on economic justice—the more I feel that I can no longer remain a bystander to certain directives from Postal Service management, whether local or national. At times, some of those directives seem to be self-destructive—even for the management itself.

In heeding this sense of a call to action, I sometimes feel that I am standing all alone. Others may complain about the problems "off the clock," but don't take a stand officially for fear of future harassment. This is especially true for part-time employees who need all the hours of work they can get. Yet someone must be willing to speak up, regardless of the cost. Otherwise, the problems will only get worse.

At this time, I have two options for action for justice in my workplace. One is to prepare through correspondence courses for a future managerial position in an area with broader responsibilities. The other is to continue to serve on the Employee Involvement/Quality Work Life committees of which I am a member representing our union.

•

Many of the employees I work with share the Christian faith. We are all concerned with justice and doing the best job we can. These men (and they are presently all men) have a special way of encouraging me— at least in private—when I speak out. They are also an important instrument God uses to call me back in line when I stray for some reason. A good case in point is the recent irritability I suffered through (or maybe they suffered through) as the result of an overburdened work load. They jokingly asked if I was going to the church communal penance service that week. Yet I knew that while they were telling me to "cool it," their joking was also an example of how they respect my faith and convictions.

Our office is staffed by a relatively small group; we number only seven. Relationships and friendships among us seem to be deeper than among those at larger offices. We had a family picnic one year and a mixed bowling team. This year we got around to making a trip to a major league baseball game. These actions allow us to put aside work tensions and see a different side of one another. Some of us meet on certain days to share lunch, faith, family concerns, and hope for the future.

One of my coworkers has just started praying with a group of friends in his hometown. He knows that I still pray with a charismatic prayer group. As we share experiences of our prayer while "casing" our routes, we nurture each other as well as witness to a third employee who is looking for a church community for himself.

•

As I continue to reflect on my career as a letter carrier—its joys, sufferings, challenges, and dreams—I realize the power and presence of God guiding my way.

There is an inscription on the old Washington, D.C., post office that summarizes well how I see myself in this ministry:

Messenger of Sympathy and Love
Servant of Parted Friends
Consoler of the Lonely
Bond of the Scattered Family
Enlarger of the Common Life
Carrier of News and Knowledge
Instrument of Trade and Industry
Promoter of Mutual Acquaintance
Of Peace and Goodwill among People and Nations.

· 13 ·

MARGARET HEBBLETHWAITE

Finding God in Dishes and Diapers

Some years ago shortly after the birth of my son, a single friend asked me how much time I spent each day feeding him. I quickly tallied up the night feeding, diaper changes, and meals that lingered because we were both content. When I said "at least four hours," my friend looked surprised.

But the hours passed quickly. If I were to choose anything in baby-minding that is the least wearing, it is feeding time. Often, I could do something else at the same time I fed my baby: I could feed and read, feed and talk, or feed and eat my own meal. On the other hand, there were those times when we were alone and I would do nothing but hold him, look at him, love him.

In those times I prayed. As I held my baby in stillness and quiet, it was a perfect time to turn to God. "I have calmed and quieted my soul, like a weaned child with its mother; my soul is like the weaned child that is with me" (Psalm 131:2). I would look at my baby and reflect: "I'm holding you, and God's holding me. I'm feeding you, and God's feeding me." It was at these moments of prayer that I began to perceive God as the source of all motherly love, giving me the warmth, safety, and nourishment I needed to hand on to my child.

Margaret Hebblethwaite is a writer in Oxford, England.

At first it was a simple thought, but it kept returning; the image was there before my eyes every time I looked at my baby. This one image spoke volumes. Did not Jesus tell us that when we pray we need not use many words, but go into our room, shut the door, and pray to God who is in secret?

•

I began to meditate more systematically about the image I had had as I held my baby: "I'm holding you, and God's holding me." I recalled many more ways that the experiences of motherhood had thrown light on God's love for us.

I remember how it felt to be pregnant. That was a perfect image of God's protection. We sometimes hear that God holds us in the palm of the hand, but how much safer it is to be in God's womb where there is no way we can fall out of God's care. God surrounds us on all sides and feeds us in perfect measure—just as a baby is nourished through the umbilical cord. We can stretch and turn, move this way and that, but we are still held warm and safe, and receive all that we need for growth.

Often when I was pregnant, I thought of the tiny creature inside me and tried to send in waves of love. Not for just four hours, but for 24 hours I was holding my child in safety and helping it grow. I could say, "You live in me, and I live in God. God gives life to me, and I give life to you."

People sometimes deny that God exists; this isn't surprising. We can't see God, who is holding and enclosing us, any more than the baby in the womb can see the mother. But one day when we are born into the next life, we will see the God who has been holding us all this time. And, like the baby and the mother who look at each other for the first time after birth, we say, "Have I known you so long but have never seen your face?"

•

Not only pregnancy but also childbirth itself holds a powerful image of our relationship with God. And heavens! What a religious experience a birth is. The moment you see your baby is a moment of truth. At these crucial moments of life or death, our priorities sort themselves out and we know what really matters. Life matters; love matters.

When our first baby burst into the light and cried for the first time, I wept for joy and said to him, "It's all right." Then my husband took him in his arms and said, "The facts are friendly." We were saying, "You're alive, we love you; nothing else matters."

•

It was not just the good and beautiful moments of motherhood that helped me find God—the serene pregnancy, the dramatic birth, the tender breastfeeding. God could also be found in the toddler tantrums and sibling jealousies, and in the bits of motherhood I could do without, as well as in those motherhood chores that were boring—like dishes and diapers.

It is fortunate I could think about finding God in the bad, because I had a rough time with the "terrible threes." My kids were pushing to see how much they could get away with. For a while I had no control or discipline. Even walking home from nursery school was a major battle as they dawdled to see how long they could delay. No doubt they were testing me to determine how much they could control me instead of my controlling them.

For a long time I tried to be understanding and patient, but I went too far; I made a mess of motherhood. At a party, someone introduced me as a supermom. But when I said, "I'm so little of a supermom that my two-year-old has been referred to a child guidance officer," they were shocked.

When I finally thought about trying to find God in the failures of motherhood, suddenly it was clear: God is the source of all that is good and loving and creative in motherhood. God, in a sense, is the perfect mother. When we fail, we can say, "Thank God I'm not the only mother my children have. When I make a mess of things, God will just have to clean it up for me."

We can find God in mothers, whether they are good mothers or bad mothers. We can say of the good mother that the qualities found in her are found in God. God is like her, only better. On the other hand, all the things missing in the not-so-good mother are found in God. God is the epitome of all she ought to be.

When our mothering is inadequate, we experience a terrible gap: something is wrong; something is missing. God fills that gap—the one and only "supermom."

•

Motherhood now has different demands for me since our youngest is 7 and our eldest 13. I no longer have to wipe their faces and bottoms, lift little feet over puddles, or hold small hands when crossing the street. No longer do I find God in daily life through the attention I once gave the children. My life no longer reflects the God who carries us in the womb or feeds us in a loving embrace. Everyday tasks are no longer those of the attentive parent whom Hosea evokes as an image for God— the parent who teaches his children to walk and takes them in his arms; who leads them with cords of human kindness, or who bends down to them and feeds them (Hosea 11:3-4).

Now I fight a battle with the kids to keep their things in order. My daily litany sounds like this: take the towels to the bathroom; put your dirty clothes in the laundry basket; return the milk to the fridge; sweep up the sugar spilled on the floor; return the scissors you borrowed; pick up the candy wrappers you left on the armchair.

"I didn't do it; it wasn't me," are constant whines. "Why do I have to do it?" If they suspect that others in the family aren't pulling their weight, it's their prerogative to sit back, too, because "it isn't fair." Or they'll agree to do something, then do nothing, with the plea that they "forgot." They may do half the job but leave the rest in a mess because they thought it was finished.

Subconsciously, they try to hassle me so much that I'll finally do the chore myself. It's a successful tactic. If I'm in a hurry, I will inevitably do their tasks—it's easier and quicker. Only when there's time to spare can I afford to see that others do their share.

Do I have awful kids? Am I a frightful nag and a fuss-pot? At their age, I was every bit as untidy as they are, but I know they must learn. If I don't spend extra time teaching them, then I will be locked into sweeping up their spilled sugar until they leave home.

•

How does God fit into all this? Where do we find God in the never-ending task of bringing order out of chaos?

Isn't that what God does in creation—brings order out of chaos? At the beginning of time, God spoke the word into primordial chaos—and there was light. God parted the waters and prepared the dry land for the Garden of Eden. It was all one gigantic labor of separating and tidying up.

I often resent the time I spend tidying the house, doing the laundry, cleaning the kitchen. I must remind myself that this is a share in God's work, this is the task of creation—sorting, tidying, ordering, bringing harmony out of chaos. This thinking gives dignity and spiritual worth to tasks that could be boring.

God's work is never ended—nor is a mother's. Creation was not just a "big bang" in the beginning; it is an ongoing labor throughout time. It includes peak moments like childbirth and the tedious, daily tasks of tidying up.

If I can encourage my children to share gradually in that ongoing work of bringing order out of chaos, then I will have passed on to them a daily share in God's creativity. I want them to grasp the concept that whatever they do—listening to the top 10, watching TV, going to the mall, grumping over homework—there is a way to find God in it.

·14·

CHRIS SATULLO

The Lord Catches Us in Our Craftiness

Editor is one of those jobs everyone has heard of, but few can really fathom. What do editors do, anyway, besides be colorful, grouse about dangling participles and swear a lot?

One of the editor's functions is to be a gatekeeper. The editor is the one who insists things belong in the paper despite the resistance of some people. The editor is also the one who resists putting things in the paper, despite the insistence of other people.

Is such work a ministry? Is it in any way even tangential to the gospel? I truly believe so, but sometimes I have a funny way of showing it.

Let me tell you two stories about me as editor and gatekeeper. At first glance, they might seem to portray me as a hypocrite, or at least mightily confused.

At a second glance, I hope they will seem emblematic of the struggle we all face to resolve the tension between faith in Jesus Christ and the civil religion of the workplace.

Chris Satullo is editor of *The Express* in Easton, Pa.

CHRIS SATULLO

•

I write a column for *The Express* newspaper in Easton, Pennsylvania. Recently, I wrote with some emotion in that column about how a newspaper should act with a sense of brotherhood, a special bond of caring, toward its readers.

The day after the column ran, a phone rang in the newsroom. It was a reader with a tale too sad to be untrue. Her husband had died a year ago, she said, tragically young. Shortly after his death, she discovered she was with child. Widowed, unable to work while taking care of a baby and another small child, she had fallen behind on the bills; now, the only way out was a bankruptcy petition. What she wanted from us, what she pleaded for, was for us not to publish any mention of her bankruptcy case.

I had to tell her I was sorry, but if the bankruptcy court in Reading sent us notice of her petition, as they have countless others, we would publish it, as we have countless others—briefly, with no fanfare, but nonetheless in irrevocable black and white.

Nice guy, huh?

•

Now, let me wind the clock back a few more weeks to a day when the world turned white in our annual blizzard. Again, my column was caught in a contradiction.

That day I carried on at length in the column about the existence of a commercial videotape called "Faces of Death," a vile exercise in which various snippets of film of real people suffering real death have been stitched together for the amusement of the perverse. Like it or not, this tape is a big mover in video stores. I don't like it and said so in sharp language in the column.

I also happened to be in charge of the front page that day. We were attempting to wrap up the paper early because of the snow, to give our drivers more time to battle the drifts. At 11 A.M., I was holding a spot for one more story: Pennsylvania's state treasurer, Budd Dwyer, was scheduled to resign his office that morning because of a bribery conviction.

Instead of resigning, Dwyer publicly committed suicide at his press conference. We found out at about 11:20, a scant 10 minutes before my deadline. The first story did not move over the Associated Press wire for about 10 minutes, and after deadline we were still waiting for a photo.

Though my first reaction to the news was a feeling of sickened shock, it was quickly supplanted by a sense of intensity and yes, excitement. Moments like this, when a big story breaks at deadline, fully test the craft of the journalist. Any journalist who tells you he or she doesn't relish those moments, no matter how awful the event that produces them, is a liar.

It was the awful photo of Dwyer with a gun in mouth that ran in our paper that day. With the publisher and managing editor hovering over my shoulder, I made the split-second determination that—as horrible as it was—the photo should be used, given the significance of the news. After that split second of moral calculus, my energies were devoted solely to getting that photo onto the page and that page onto the press. That was my job—to put a face of death on page A-1, while deploring them on page A-4.

•

To any journalist, those two split-second but echoing decisions—to reject a troubled woman, to accept a troubling photo—can be reconciled rather easily with the canons of the craft. If you publish a certain kind of news like bankruptcies, you must publish it consistently, without regard to the social status of the subject. Besides, in newsrooms, we've all learned that the fraudulent are as adept at telling sob stories as the truly injured.

Dwyer's suicide was a major news event. Most newspeople would agree that their job was to report it prominently, in a way that conveyed, rather than ignored, how shocking and awful it was.

But, in the realm of faith, the canons of journalism are weightless. All that matters is the word of God.

•

As a newcomer to my present church, I have been struck by how hard the congregation works to make the connection between faith and daily life, between what people do Sunday in church and what they do the rest of the week. That quest makes faith more fulfilling, but also more dangerous, because it can no longer be safely compartmentalized. My church teaches that witness is not just a weekend hobby; it is just as important around the office water cooler as at the communion rail.

Just as important—but harder. In the workplace, there is more ambiguity, more distraction. There are more false gods, false values, more temptations to be like the Pharisees of the Gospel (John 9:1-13, 28-38).

When I think about that Gospel verse, I have to confess how very like the Pharisees I sometimes am in my work as an editor.

The Pharisees are men of rules who seek to tame the frightful moral and emotional ambiguity of living by reducing holiness and morality to a set of formal policies. They like things neat. A right way, a wrong way. A villain, and a hero (usually themselves). No painful mysteries that prove to be occasions of grace.

If, for example, a blind man (or a woman in bankruptcy) came to them in need, they would offer these people not help, but rules. "Sorry, fella, no healing on the Sabbath" or "Sorry, Ma'am, it's against our policy."

The Pharisees also are, like any good reporter, professional skeptics. When an event occurs that rattles their worldview, such as a blind man gaining sight on the Sabbath, they suspect fraud and seek to sniff it out with a worthy investigative zeal. They are ruthless in discounting the testimony of a man they consider to be an unreliable source—a mere beggar.

The irony of this Gospel, of course, is that it is these Pharisees who are blind, while the blind man sees Jesus clearly and proclaims him Lord.

What blinds the Pharisees is their faith in their own righteousness and wisdom, in their limited worldview.

•

The workplaces of America are full of Pharisees, people, often well-meaning, whose vision of the Gospel is obstructed by their loyalty to the religion of their craft, their work.

Make no mistake—the workplace is this nation's great, unrecognized church; each workplace, each profession has its own culture, its own set of values. They are largely unexamined, but they are relentlessly inculcated, relentlessly enforced. For many, this religion is more persuasive, more powerful than anything they observe on Sunday. It can become a false god we place before the real one.

•

Some rotten people work at newspapers and do very well in the eyes of the world. And, sometimes, to do well in the eyes of my workplace, I do rotten things, like running photos on the front page that many people find offensive. My civil religion can be at war with the Gospel.

Is the conflict hopeless? Are the canons of my craft nothing more than a false god that pulls me away from the Gospel?

I don't think so, or I wouldn't be in the business or love it so. No matter how often my work seems to others, or to myself, to be a grubby enterprise, to be a matter of harping, indeed feasting, upon the misfortune of others, I still see in it an opportunity for Christian witness.

•

The potential for holiness can reside in what seems utterly humble, hopelessly mundane. In the book of Samuel, for example, David, the youngest son of Jesse—the one everyone overlooked because he was assigned the "scut" work of tending the sheep—proves to be God's anointed. In John's Gospel, a blind beggar is the only person capable of recognizing and proclaiming the Good News.

Scripture reminds us constantly that, as God's people, we are called to a holiness that emulates God's holiness. But this holiness does not amount to an austere withdrawal from the world. That is the easy way out.

To heal a blind man, Jesus didn't raise his eyes aloft and whisper a prayer. He spat on the ground and then got his hands dirty making clay.

In the same way, we are to risk venturing into a fallen, broken world, getting its muck all over our hands, but somehow turning that muck into gold.

We must, in other words, make our work our witness, our ministry. To do that, we must judge the canons of our craft, our workplace religion, in the light of the Gospel; in that light, they will either be redeemed or revealed as false gods.

•

I do see redeeming value in my work.

There is a passage in Leviticus that says to the people of God: "You shall not render an unjust judgment; you shall not be partial to the poor or defer to the great: with justice you shall judge your neighbor. You shall not go around as a slanderer among your people" (Lev. 19:15).

When I read those words, I see a pretty fair description of a good journalist. That makes me feel pretty good about what I do.

But, still, but still . . . the Lord catches us in our craftiness.

He reminds us, with a phone call from a desperate woman, with the destructive act of a desperate man, that the fit of faith and craft are not always perfect. We assume that they are at the peril of our souls.

Our work culture and Jesus' clarion call to a difficult holiness do collide—frequently in some professions, occasionally in all.

It is hard to know what to do at these moments of collision. It is hard even to recognize them for what they are. So rarely is the equation clear-cut—this way the gospel, that way the blindness of human wisdom—and you have so little time to weigh the moral calculus. Sometimes, as the snowflakes fall and deadline approaches, you have only seconds.

It is a huge daily struggle, but it is the struggle we are called upon to undertake. Each day we must examine the religion of our workplace and nudge it a little closer toward the gospel, at least in the way we work, if not in the way our colleagues do.

This struggle is more than we, in our worldly wisdom, can manage by ourselves. We require, first of all, the grace of God, and secondly, the help and support of a community of faith.

Without those, as we go to work each day, we are simply wanderers in a confused and broken land.

With them, we can be people on the mission of the Gospel.

Let us pray for God's grace, and let us, by all means, help one another.

· 15 ·

CECELIA NEWBOLD

To Walk with Each One

As a young woman I chose a career in nursing—considering what was expected of me and weighing these expectations against my abilities and potentialities. But until I was actually involved in a clinical situation, I couldn't evaluate my strength of ability or purpose. As time went on, I discovered that as a nurse I was more than a therapeutic agent or a liaison between doctor and patient—but was a close confidant of personal information, a participant rather than just an observer in a patient's life, a mother image, a physical contact with the living world (to the dying), a teacher and a friend. Through the years many of the lessons my patients taught me have been a resource to draw upon; their testing of my abilities has strengthened my purpose; their life-sharing relationships have been a ministry to me.

•

In a hospital situation, it is necessary to know how to deal with conflict in many forms. Patients frequently are in conflict with themselves, their feelings, their reactions to pain, to disease, to illness. They may be irritated with the service and action of the medical staff and with other patients. Illness and hospitalization put stresses on family relationships, and at times there may be painful conflicts with those they love. Working

---

Cecelia Newbold is a registered nurse in Denver, Colo.

with these realities gives a nurse insight into causes and effects of conflicts that apply also outside a hospital.

•

In the past, my nursing has taken me into the arenas of the army, doctor's office, hospital, and private duty. To avoid obsolescence during the years when my children were very small, it was necessary to maintain an interested outlook and an active curiosity in nursing trends. The field of nursing is ever-widening to include specialties such as coronary care with electronic monitoring equipment, aero-space medicine, research, etc., but there are still many patients who require professional bedside care by general duty or private duty nurses.

Nursing is an art as well as a science. It is not a field of self-sacrifice, but rather an area of ministry to others that gives the greatest personal satisfaction. People need people, not only to meet their own needs but to be needed by others. The relationship of patient and nurse is unlike any other, and a part of its uniqueness is the intimacy with which one relates to a person. It is in this dimension—sharing another's concerns by serving the whole person—that bedside nursing brings immeasurable rewards.

Because of additional responsibilities I have assumed in my church and community, my institutional nursing has been somewhat limited in recent months. I call my current nursing "bouquet nursing" and "bottom of the barrel nursing."

Bouquet nursing is the term I use for caring for a friend or acquaintance for an eight-hour shift (or several) following surgery or in a period of crisis. I feel that professional bedside nursing is the gift I can best give, and this is my "bouquet of flowers." In order to do this, I always consult with the friend (or family) and check with the doctor and floor supervisor. I indicate my non-paid nursing status and have a clear understanding with the staff in regard to duties to assume or share with the nursing team assigned to the patient.

Bottom-of-the-barrel nursing is the result of an arrangement with a nearby hospital to the effect that when they have exhausted the nursing registry list and their reserve list, they call me. When they call, I know they are "scraping the bottom of the barrel" and that it is a critical situation. They respect my wishes to be called only as a last resort, and I make every effort to arrange my affairs to respond to their call.

As I review many of my past bottom-of-the-barrel cases, I find that almost all were critical, emergency, or terminal. Because each case begins in crisis, I have a particularly close relationship with my patients and their families. There is a communication between nurse and critical patient unlike that in any other relationship. Doctors may see their patients on hospital rounds for a few minutes in the morning and evening; family may visit for many hours, but this is an emotional stress on both patient and family. The nurse spends eight hours in a special dimension of "caring." I have learned to adapt myself readily wherever I am and whatever I'm doing. My patient is an essential part of my life for the time I'm on his or her case.

●

Many patients (and their families) enter the hospital feeling that pain is punishment or penalty, and that death is the ultimate punishment. Some people never accept the fact that pain is universal and that everyone feels pain, though reactions differ. Since pain cannot be separated from emotions, it is not enough to give medications. Pain must be "managed" by certain nursing techniques and arts, and by giving emotional support and strength. Patients need help to understand their pain and their reaction of anxiety and hostility to it.

One of the major concerns of the patient and his or her family is the imminence of death. It is apparent to me that most people, no matter what their religious background, are inadequately prepared for the ultimate fact of death for themselves and their families. The church— both clergy and laity—needs a better understanding and interpretation of the Christian hope. Some preparation is essential if the message of the gospel is to have any significance at times of crisis.

Although as a nurse I am not required to provide a spiritual ministry to patients, to ignore a patient's religious background or relationship to God would do a disservice to the whole person. I need an awareness of the meaning of religion to support the patient in his or her use of religious beliefs. I must accept the differences in religious beliefs and realize the influence of my religious beliefs in dealing with my patients.

•

I have always felt that a comatose patient is much more aware of what is said and done in his or her presence than has been believed in the past. I talk to my unconscious patients. I greet them when I come into their rooms, tell them my name, and express aloud the hope that I can serve to make them more comfortable and to regain their health. When I turn a patient for nursing procedures, treatment, or medication, I say what I'm going to do, that there may be some discomfort, but that this procedure will help to make him or her more comfortable or aid in the recovery. During the day, I tell the patient of the beauty of the day, the view from the window, the loveliness of the flowers in the room. I request all visitors to speak only the words they would want such patients to hear, for I believe they can hear.

Not long ago, I had a patient who had attempted suicide by an overdose of drugs. She was in a deep coma and had not responded to any stimuli or therapy, and her prognosis was guarded. When I came on the case, the resident physician indicated that the patient had been comatose for a long time and that not much hope was held for her recovery.

As I cared for the patient that day, I talked to her from time to time in a quiet voice about one of the Greek Islands in the Aegean Sea, which is a favorite place of mine. I suggested that if she were to walk with me up that heather-covered hill, we could see the entire island. So I described the feel of the rough textured heather on our legs as we walked through it. I described the color of the heather plants and the pungent fragrance. I tried to convey the feeling of the warmth of the sun and the clear sweet air so characteristic of Greece. I told her of the inhabitants of the island, the little donkeys and peacocks, and how their voices were intermingled with the sea sounds and buzzing of insects. And then we "walked" down the other side of the hill, under the olive trees and onto the white sand, and stood looking out at the incredibly blue sea.

For the first time since her admittance, the woman began to move. Her legs moved in a rhythmic way. Her knee would bend and the leg extend, and then the other, and they moved alternately. I realized she was "walking."

In time this woman recovered and went home. I saw her from a distance once and wondered if she had any memories of hearing about the little Greek island of Moni.

•

A few years ago, while visiting in Turkey, I entered the tower room of an old military fort in Uskadar. This had been the quarters Florence Nightingale had used during the Crimean War when she and 37 nurses cared for British soldiers in this installation. Her room is unlocked only a few times during the year for an occasional visitor. The musty room held only a desk and some pictures of the "Angel of the Crimea," a bouquet of dead flowers (sent several months before on the anniversary of her birthday), and a few letters and diaries she had written. As I leafed through the fragile pages, one phrase in her handwriting caught my eye: "To be a good nurse one must first be a good woman." To be a nursing Christian (or a Christian nurse), to meet a person's physiological and psychological needs—whether patient, neighbor, friend, or stranger, to care for life and inevitable death is a lifetime challenge. It requires a fine skill that can never be perfected. In a sense, every Christian must meet the same challenge: to meet the needs of others, to minister to them with the abilities and skills that are part of the equipment of each one of us.

·16·

ED WOJCICKI

Overbooked and Overwhelmed

The frantic pace that is chewing up American society is also swallowing many dedicated people involved in the church and in social justice causes. People are overbooked, but the phone keeps ringing, delivering unwelcome news about another new committee or another meeting. Even people who understand this is happening don't know how to control it. It's crazy.

The irony is that as some people expand into more and more causes, they accomplish less of lasting value. Then a bit of desperation creeps in, plus a little self-pity. The result of doing all this work for God is that people feel angry and frustrated and probably somewhat bitter because nobody seems to care how hard they're working.

●

For me, the problem is not bitterness (not yet, anyway) but that so many important things go undone. Priorities unravel. Relationships suffer. People call or drop by, and I say "uh-huh" a few times; and a few seconds after they hang up or leave I realize that I had been giving them only a tiny percentage of my conscious attention—that is, if I heard them at all.

Ed Wojcicki is editor of *The Catholic Times* in Springfield, Ill.

In those moments of conversation, I became incapable of shifting gears. I neglected to rejoice with those who were trying to rejoice and failed to show compassion for those who were moaning or mourning right in front of me. I've done this even to good friends and close family members.

●

One week in January, for example, I attended a local Martin Luther King Jr. commemorative breakfast on Monday (the scheduled federal holiday), a nuclear-disarmament meeting Wednesday night, and then a right-to-life rally Sunday in connection with the 15th anniversary of *Roe v. Wade.* (All great causes, I believe.)

Meanwhile, I also had to face my 8-year-old daughter, who with great accuracy keeps track of when and how often I'm gone. The preservation of the family is a social justice issue, too; but every day, yes, every day when I get home from work, my children ask me if I have a meeting that night. Shouldn't that tell me something?

Even more piercing is when the children ask, "Are you going to be our baby-sitter tonight?" Heck no! I'm no baby-sitter—I'm their daddy!

●

The only cure for being overbooked and overwhelmed is to make a series of concrete, conscious decisions to change my own behavior.

A good first step is having the humility to say no once in a while. This is initially very, very difficult for dedicated workers, but it gets a bit easier when I realize organizations can get along nicely without my every brilliant insight. I wonder: Don't I trust, really trust, that the Spirit is working through other people, just as the Spirit's always nudging me?

Another need in relationships is to encourage friends and coworkers to relax. All too often I do the opposite by teasing others that every minute not spent working is a minute wasted. This leads to an unhealthy kind of tacit competition in which I keep a jealous eye on others' productivity—and then exhaust myself trying to keep up with unrealistic expectations that I myself have created.

●

Perhaps in my anxiety to do so many good works—presumably for God—I actually shut out opportunities for God to work as passionately as possible in my life and in my community.

Perhaps God is calling in the night with a suggestion or a solution, but I'm too busy burning the midnight oil to hear it. Taking the time to be nourished in prayer and refreshed in recreation may take more discipline than planning the next agenda or participating in the next informational meeting about Star Wars.

●

People caught in the trap of feeling unreasonably obligated to show up for every good cause need to learn to escape from overcommitment. When they're up to their eyebrows in frustration, some of what they do is counterproductive anyway. No one can work for long out of true Christian compassion while ensnared in the trap that so easily breeds bitterness and despair.

The challenge is to gain a new sense of freedom without giving up. Jesus has already saved the world. So my job is not to do the same but to serve him by using my gifts effectively today, praying for the grace to choose my causes wisely, and leaving the outcome up to God and my fellow sojourners.

·17·

HERMAN LOEWEN

When I Went Broke

It is August 10, 1981. I get up at 6:30 in the morning.

I ride an exercise bike, do some calisthenics, take a sauna and shower, and dress for work. I eat breakfast with my family. Everyone has plans for the day.

I go to work. I review the achievements of yesterday. I check with my department heads about the activities for the day. I do all the things a business executive does. I meet with customers, other businesspeople and civic officials. I participate in committee meetings. I go out for lunch using a company credit card. If my car needs servicing or washing, I pick up the phone and ask one of my employees to see to it.

At suppertime, I go home to my wife and family—who have been busy doing important and fun things. They are not working for wages or tied to specific hours.

In the evening we go out or have friends in and have a relaxed time in the comfort of a family room with a warm fireplace in our dream home. We reminisce about a recent trip. We plan for the next vacation. Where will we go? We can make plans. Things are stable and predictable.

Our mortgage payments are reasonable and can easily be met out of my paycheck. Oh, we can always use more money. I complain about

---

Herman Loewen is a salesperson for the Manufacturers Life Insurance Company in Winnipeg, Manitoba, Canada.

high taxes and high prices, but I can do all the things I really want to do.

•

That evening, the banker phones. He wants to see me in my office at eight in the morning.

I meet him. He is there with his lawyer, the receiver and the bailiff. The lawyer reads the demand. "Can you pay off your loan in the next hour?" How many people could repay their operating loan in that time? I couldn't. There had been no previous mention of foreclosure. The receiver asks me to call my employees together. He fires every one. The bailiff changes the lock. They take my car. They accompany me to my house to pick up my wife's car. By 9:30 P.M. the same day, 40 years of hard work, all my dreams, my future and my retirement are gone.

I have no income.

I have no place to work.

I have no status.

No one wants me.

Suddenly I realize I have no money. I have no job. The only vehicle I have is a car I bought for my teenage daughter a few months ago. I will lose our home.

Everything I've worked for is gone.

My employees are paid their salaries and vacation pay. I get nothing.

•

What will I do?

I am angry and ashamed.

I am a failure.

My pride is hurt.

I am disappointed with people, the church, and friends.

I question and even blame God.

I wonder about my faith.

How much suffering can I take and survive?

•

I have run a successful business in Steinbach, often called Manitoba's "automobile city." I have won many awards for running a highly efficient business. Fewer than 10 General Motors dealers have won the President's Triple Crown four years in succession; my dealership did. I was the first and probably the only Canadian auto dealer to take part in the annual convention of the National Automobile Association in the United States.

Now I am bankrupt. Broke. Financially, emotionally, I have nothing.

I take stock.

What can I do?

Where will we live?

How can I face the future?

I have only a few years left to work. How will I manage retirement?

•

If I had died, my insurance would have paid all my debts. My family would not have had to suffer a bleak future because of me.

My family was very supportive. One of our daughters moved in with another daughter and son-in-law. At least in my daughter's apartment my wife and I had a place to live. We had privacy.

My wife found a job and was working within two weeks.

I asked around for a career opportunity. One friend invited me out for lunch. He told me his company would not hire me. I would be too difficult to manage. I was too independent. Their company was too structured. Sorry.

He suggested I take a position with an insurance firm that had shown interest in me. Within a few weeks I was studying toward my license to become an insurance agent.

I failed.

I thought I could read English. I found I read in "Automotive." The exam was written in "Insurance." There is no similarity.

With more studying, I was able to pass the test in three more weeks. My training allowance started. I made a few sales. I was able to earn a living—not enough to support my family, but along with my wife's salary enough to get by.

Please picture my wife, whom I love dearly, who has helped me in my career, entertained my business friends, kept up with current affairs—a person who has raised our five children, often alone. She has

107

spent all her time making my life comfortable, enjoyable, and worth-while.

She has not worked at a job outside the home for more than 30 years. Her skills are outdated; her hours have been flexible. She now has to adjust to learning a new job. How do you get new skills at age 51? She has to adjust to day and evening shifts. Her life is completely upset.

Our one daughter at home was going into grade 12. She did not want to change schools. She did not want to leave her friends. Her life is so completely changed.

Time is a healer. Not great, but a healer.

Now we have our own apartment.

My wife bought a car, but it wasn't easy. Our dealership was only 30 days past due on accounts payable, but when I wanted to finance my wife's car through the General Motors Acceptance Corporation they refused. They said my credit was no good and my wife had no credit rating. Another large GM dealer went to bat for us. He told GMAC that if Herman Loewen couldn't buy a car from him and finance it with GMAC, then they were too small to handle his business. Needless to say, they decided to provide the financing, and I paid ahead of schedule in just over a year.

•

My new job is beginning to make sense. My wife, on the other hand, still is not settled in her career. Because of budget controls, she has had to change responsibilities several times at the hospital where she works.

We had good Christian friends who were genuinely concerned about us. A couple of these friends got together and appointed one person to make sure I would have money available to pay expenses while I worked out the mess and found a job. They made it easy to draw money and tried to make it as pleasant as possible. Fortunately, I did not have to accept this help. It felt good to know that people cared, but I was able to make it on my own. I needed to develop as much self-esteem as possible. I had none at the time.

I had always thought of myself as a caring Christian, but the bankruptcy taught me a few things firsthand. I have a better handle on how to be more caring to a hurting neighbor. I think all of us care about our fellow Christians. We would really like to do something that will relieve suffering. But many of us do not know how to express our concern. I don't have all the answers, but I do have a few suggestions.

Don't avoid the person who is hurting, even if you aren't sure of the proper thing to say. I remember one person who would leave church by the side door to make sure he wouldn't have to talk to me. That hurt.

Be sincere. Surely this does not have to be faked.

Practice helps improve expertise. Many people are experiencing hard times of one kind or another. Think of what will really help. Many of us avoid involvement because we think we'll have to shell out money. But the real help is more often emotional than monetary.

People around us have many hurts. Bereavements, financial loss, wayward children, illness and so on. Whether you are hurting because of a broken leg, a kidney stone, or a migraine headache does not matter. You hurt. You are sick. You want relief. We can often help a lot by learning how to approach people, quietly shake a hand, touch someone, perhaps just be there.

●

Do you know of someone who has lost a child or has a child who has a disability? How about someone who is struggling with a strained marriage? Or someone who is trying to make sense out of a wayward son or daughter?

Here are some questions you can answer for yourself.

After I have visited the person in question, is he or she better off? Do I feel better? Or both?

Are we sometimes tempted to blame people for their own problems? Do we sometimes think that if they had not been so foolish, if they had some backbone or if they would stop feeling sorry for themselves they could rise above their problems? Some of that may be true, but dwelling on it at this time is not helpful.

Go out of your way to express your concern. It is better to say the wrong thing in love than to avoid the hurting person. Remember that he or she also does not know what to reply.

By all means pray for the person, but don't leave it at that. Offer a job to the unemployed, time and love to the bereaved, sympathy to the parents with wayward children, baby-sitting to the parents with a disabled child.

Do not highlight your success in the area of the person's struggle. A person who is concerned about a child does not need stories about how well your children have applied themselves. A person who is losing a business does not need to hear how profitable you are.

•

I realize that unless you have personally experienced hardship or any other socially unacceptable failure, you cannot really understand how the suffering person feels. I am just as guilty in not taking time or constructive action with hurting people, and I know better.

There are no easy or quick cure answers. If we would follow the advice given by Jesus Christ we would do well: Love your neighbor as yourself—not because he or she is easy to love, but because Christ loves you.

And furthermore, "What does it profit, my brothers and sisters, if you say you have faith but do not have works? Can faith save you? If a brother or sister is naked and lacks daily food, and one of you says to them, 'Go in peace; keep warm and eat your fill,' and yet you do not supply their daily needs, what is the good of that? So faith by itself, if it has no works, is dead" (James 2:14-16).

PART
• III •

HOW CAN THE CHURCH
SUPPORT THE SPIRITUALITY
OF MY WORK?

· 18 ·

DAVIDA FOY CRABTREE

They Bring Their Work
to Church

I once stood outside an Asian temple shrine and looked at all the shoes
of the believers lined up by the door. Shoes that had come from offices
and marketplaces, from homes and fishing boats, from fields and factories, all left at the door as the believers entered a holy place.

Christian churches seldom ask people to leave their shoes at the
door. Yet we often seem to ask people to leave their lives at the door
when they come to worship. We invite them to shed their cares and
enter a holy place where God will accept them just as they are. All too
often we offer worship that they do not experience as connected to their
daily lives. The chasm between Sunday and Monday seems to them
unbridgeable.

The shoes outside that temple door have haunted me as a pastor.
I have wanted to find ways believers could bring all of their lives to
worship, and all of their faith into the rest of their lives. That is the
teaching of the church of Jesus Christ: that no ground is more holy,
no work more sacred, no life more worthy than any other. Every moment, every place and every interaction is sacred and holy, infused with
the Spirit's presence.

The Rev. Davida Foy Crabtree is the senior minister at Colchester Fed-
erated Church in Colchester, Conn.

•

Some years ago, a number of the laity and I as pastor in our church began to have some conversations about a set of problems revolving around faith issues: lack of interest in Bible study, unwillingness to talk about one's personal faith, failure to give explicitly Christian consideration to decisions the church faced, the absence of leadership in the church. It became clear to us that the central issue was the inability of the laity to integrate their faith with their lives, and the failure of the church to develop a program to help them with that central task.

The church's traditional answer to its members' need for a faith that would sustain them Monday through Saturday has been Bible study, personal devotions, and faithful attendance at worship. We decided to take a new approach.

We decided to concentrate for a few years on learning about the daily lives of our members. Instead of assuming that we knew what their needs were and knew what would meet those needs, we would listen to them intently on their terms. No more Bible studies to which only a handful would come. No more traditional programs in devotional life. The church and its pastor would stop teaching and start learning.

•

Three members formed a listening team and invited parishioners to come together in occupational groups to talk about their work lives. The listening team led the members in discussion and I served as silent observer and recorder.

Those sessions led to the formation of an ongoing support group for laity who wanted to connect faith and their work, and specifically to explore ministry in the workplace. Their bimonthly program included personal sharing, reflection on the workplace and ministry, reading a book together, and—of all things—Bible study and theological reflection.

We discovered an important principle. By beginning with their lives, we were validating the authority of the laity and empowering them to reflect on the faith. When we had begun with Bible study and theology, we had started on ground where the clergy had authority. For laity who have been unchurched, or whose Christian education was lacking in the fundamentals of the faith, such an approach was threatening. They assumed that everyone else was biblically literate and that they would be revealing their ignorance, so they avoided any such situations.

When we begin with their lives, however, we begin where they have authority. We provide an opportunity for them to talk about their work and to reflect on the impact of that work on the rest of their lives. As they develop confidence and trust, they begin to ask theological questions and to wrestle with the Scriptures. The church's interest in their daily life gave both church and life new dimension.

•

We offered some daylong conferences and weekend retreats to the whole congregation on themes related to the ministries of the laity: "Beyond a Sunday Christianity," "Discovering Your Gifts," "Personality and Work: Who I Am and What I Do." A new support group started up even as the first continued.

As pastor, I began to visit people at their workplaces. In some cases, I "shadowed" members for an entire workday, simply observing and later reflecting with them on the experience.

•

We began to include a new prayer in our time of worship. During the service each week, visual reminders of a different occupation graced the communion table or the pulpit rail. We invited members who had ever done that particular kind of work to stand during the prayer. Those who were currently employed in that line of work received a letter two weeks earlier inviting them to worship and asking for their suggestions for the prayer. Their words were used as much as possible in composing the prayers. The various visual reminders were solicited by a member of the Diaconate from members of the occupation group.

Our sanctuary is classic New England with large expanses of clear windows and good lighting. On the communion table are a brass cross and offering plates. The table sits directly in front of and below our large, mid-height central pulpit. Any item on the table is at the focal point of the service.

115

Here are some examples of prayers:

1. Builders and Contractors (On the communion table: level, saw, lumber, T-square)

   Creator God, the scriptures are full of your image as Builder and of your mandates to us when we would build. We ask your blessing this day on all who are builders and contractors by trade or profession. Inspire them with commitment to quality and safety, with a right care for their workers, and with the fortitude to make it through times of no work and little pay. Help them balance their many loyalties—to contracts, to customers, to workers, to suppliers, to laws, and to their own families and selves. May they know and find their ministries in the footsteps of the carpenter of Nazareth. In his name we pray, Amen.

2. Mechanics (On the communion table: large tool box with its shelves open and full of wrenches and other tools)

   Eternal God, you above all know the challenge of keeping things running. We pray today for the mechanics of our world who repair and rebuild the machines the rest of us wear down and wear out. Grant them pride in their work, integrity, patience, and persistence in keeping up with advances in technology. Encourage them, O God, in a sense of ministry in the name of Jesus Christ as they contribute to our safety and productivity, and as they work and serve. Amen.

3. Bookkeepers (On the communion table: account books, computer paper, pencils)

   O good and gracious God, we hold before you in prayer this morning all who are bookkeepers, and ask that you might grant them compassion, a sense of humor, and patience, both with detail and with people. Give them a knowledge of their ministry with Jesus Christ as they strive for accuracy and as they interact with all whose records they keep. And, O God, in that great book which you keep, may their names be inscribed for their faithfulness. Amen.

4. Seamstresses/Tailors (On the communion table: a sewing machine and fabric)

Gracious God, like a seamstress you have pieced us together, bound us at our raw edges and pulled the gathering thread of faith through all our lives to make us one. And so we trust that you will receive our prayers for these who stand before you, the seamstresses and tailors who turn finished product from raw material, who press and stitch, and pin and baste to achieve perfection in their work. In this day of clothing off the rack and draperies off the shelf, bless them in their craft and grant them the knowledge of their many opportunities to minister in their dealings with people, their creativity, and their careful work. In Christ's name. Amen.

•

Many of our members have spoken to me of the powerful experience of seeing the symbols of their work lives laid out before the cross. For others, the power was in the sense of blessing that came as they stood and we prayed for them. Some were unable to be present on "their" day, and would ask for a copy of the prayer.

Frequently I would see a member in the supermarket or on the street and he or she would stop me to say how meaningful the prayer that week had been. Often it was not because it was for their own work, but because they had had a new insight about the way others minister in their daily work.

On reflection, it seems that we accomplished far more than we intended. Not only did we help members begin to bridge between Sunday and Monday, but we helped them understand one another. We brought their workday lives into worship, and in the process began to bridge public and private worlds.

The liturgical innovation became the basis for a strengthened pastoral ministry. Yet there are many ways the traditional liturgy can also reflect a concern for ministries in daily life. Baptism, Holy Communion, and reception of new members are moments of deep connection to the ministry of all Christians. All too often, however, we clergy assume the connection between liturgy and daily life is clear when it is not the least bit clear to the laity. We tend to use indirect, conceptual, ideational ways of expressing the connection. The laity of my church have taught us the importance of direct, concrete expression—although I am sure I still have not learned how to do it!

Even our calls to worship can make a difference to the way Christians perceive the relation between their daily lives and the Gospel ministry to which we are all called. If we always begin by inviting them to leave the cares of the world outside the door, like the shoes outside the temple, we may be fostering a "sanctuary Christianity" that truncates their faith. If, however, we invite them to bring to worship every aspect of their lives, laying them before the cross, worshipers can be helped to bridge that gap between Sunday and Monday and to live the faith more richly and fully.

Credits and Sources of Articles

"Confronting Dualism" by William Diehl is adapted in part from the annual Mark Gibbs lecture in 1989 sponsored by *Laity Exchange*. Used by permission of *Laity Exchange* and the author.

"The Spirituality of Everyday Life" by Hal Miller. Copyright © 1989, *Voices in the Wilderness*, P.O. Box 4486, Salem, MA 01870. Used by permission of the author.

"Andy's Diner" by Jeff Behrens appeared in the *National Catholic Reporter*, Kansas City, Mo., July 28, 1989. Used by permission of the author.

"Finding the Courage to Take Risks" by Frank Macchiarola appeared as "Prayer and the Pursuit of Public Virtue." Copyright © 1987, *Commonweal Foundation*, 15 Dutch Street, New York, NY 10038. Used by permission of the publisher.

"Our Task Is to Create Worlds" by Emil Antonucci. Copyright © 1989, *Commonweal Foundation*, 15 Dutch Street, New York, NY 10038. Used with permission of the publisher.

"I Am a Building Tradesman" by Peter Terzick appeared in *Home Is a Time as Much as a Place*. Copyright © 1988, United Brotherhood of

"The Lord Catches Us in Our Craftiness" by Chris Satullo appeared as "Grey Areas in Black Type" in *Action Information*. Reprinted by permission from The Alban Institute, 4125 Nebraska Avenue, NW, Washington, DC, 20016. Copyright © 1987. All rights reserved.

"To Walk with Each One" by Cecelia Newbold is adapted from *My Job and My Faith* edited by Frederick Wentz. Copyright © 1967 Abingdon Press, Nashville, Tenn., 1967. Used by permission of the publisher. All rights reserved.

"Overbooked and Overwhelmed" by Ed Wojcicki appeared as "I'm Just a Guy Who Can't Say No" in *Salt*, Chicago, Ill., March 1988. Used by permission of the author.

"When I Went Broke" by Herman Loewen appeared in *The Marketplace*, Winnipeg, Manitoba, May/June 1989. Used by permission of the publisher.

"They Bring Their Work to Church" by Davida Foy Crabtree appeared in *Action Information*. Reprinted by permission from The Alban Institute, 4125 Nebraska Avenue, Washington, D.C. 20016. Copyright © 1990. All rights reserved.

Acknowledgments

I never could have edited this book if I had not been blessed with the opportunity to serve as president of the National Center for the Laity, based in Chicago. This organization of Catholics committed to "promoting the vocation of the laity in and to the world" has kept the idea alive in my own church that the primary role of the laity is in our daily work: on our job, with our family, and in our community. I am especially thankful to my mentors in this organization, Russell Barta and Ed Marciniak.

I also must thank my friend and colleague Bill Droel. It was he who first sparked my interest in the spirituality of work, and he continues to offer me fresh insights and challenges into what it means to be a Christian in the world.

Several people from different denominations read and commented on an early draft of this book. I thank these people for their time, their suggestions, and their support: John Docker of the Episcopal Church, Bill Droel of the National Center for the Laity, Susan Gillies of the American Baptist Church, Sally Simmel of the Evangelical Lutheran Church in America, and Nelvin Vos of *Laity Exchange*.

In terms of ecumenical dialogue and leadership on the issue of faith and work, no one compares with Bill Diehl. He has been unceasing in his efforts to convince both his own and all the other Christian denominations that the support of the ministry of daily life is a critical element of the church's mission. I am proud and honored that he was willing to contribute the foreword to this book.

ACKNOWLEDGMENTS

Of course, this book could not have existed if the articulate authors of the book's articles had not taken the time to reflect on the spirituality of their work. I thank them for allowing their articles to be included and for trusting me to edit and arrange them.

I also want to recognize Bob Moluf and Irene Getz, Augsburg Fortress Publishers, as well as my partner in ACTA Publications, Mary Buckley, for sharing the vision to embark on this new series, *The Christian at Work in the World*. The editing and production skills of Stefanie Cox and Steve Aggergaard have brought our joint efforts to fruition.

We hope that this series will begin to fill a need for primary material on the experience of Christians trying to live out their faith in their daily lives.

The four people who help me do that more than anyone else are my wife, Kathy, and our three children, Abby, Nate, and Zack. I thank them most of all.